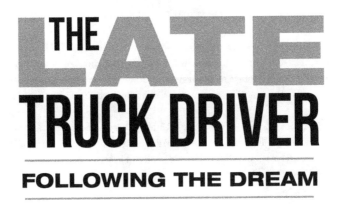

THE LATE
TRUCK DRIVER

FOLLOWING THE DREAM

DAVID LONGANECKER

ARCHWAY
PUBLISHING

Archway Publishing books may be ordered through booksellers or by contacting:

Archway Publishing
1663 Liberty Drive
Bloomington, IN 47403
www.archwaypublishing.com
844-669-3957

ISBN: 978-1-6657-0114-3 (sc)
ISBN: 978-1-6657-0113-6 (hc)
ISBN: 978-1-6657-0115-0 (e)

Library of Congress Control Number: 2021902111

Print information available on the last page.

Archway Publishing rev. date: 02/02/2021

CONTENTS

ACKNOWLEDGMENTS

I AM INDEBTED to many for assisting me to follow my retirement dream of driving a truck. I thank Aims Community College for squeezing me into their commercial truck-driving course on an overload basis. Thanks, as well, to Swift Transportation, which took a chance on hiring a rather "mature" fellow as a driver, and Ed Gomez, my mentor driver at Swift, for teaching me the real rules of the road and for great camaraderie during our five weeks together. Most significantly, however, thanks to my wonderful wife, Mary Jane, who helped me keep my truck-driving dream alive during my first career. She also endured my long absences while driving and my incessant chatter about the joys of driving when I was home. She even joined me on some of my travels during my brief but joyous career as a professional truck driver, and she contributed the chapter that provides the somewhat different perspective on truck driving from a spouse's point of view.

CHAPTER 1
WHAT GOT ME HERE

SATURDAY, SEPTEMBER 17: This morning, I took the final three steps of the exams to become an over-the-road truck driver, passing the precheck, skills test, and road tests required to receive a Class A commercial driving license (CDL). I won't have the actual license until Monday, when I go to the Colorado Department of Motor Vehicles (DMV) to present my paperwork. But as of today, I'm a legit truck driver.

Before discussing today, however, I want to describe what got me to this point (including the rationale for this missive's title) and the various steps that led up to today.

With respect to the title *The Late Truck Driver,* obviously it isn't about a deceased truck driver—or I wouldn't be writing it. Nor is it about a truck driver who arrives late to pick up or deliver his load. As will become clear later on, you can't arrive late and be a successful truck driver; if you arrive late, you get fired. Rather, this book is about a truck driver who came late to the occupation.

Three months ago, I retired from a wonderful and rewarding career of public service, working in and leading state, regional, and national organizations involved in public policy and higher education. I enjoyed my career a great deal but chose to retire when I was young enough and spry enough to also enjoy other pursuits that had been impossible to engage in while in my original career because of the demands and attention it required.

Very high among those other desired pursuits had been an enduring dream of becoming a truck driver. Many of my friends and former colleagues have asked me how I came to this passion, most often with some wonderment of whether I had lost my mind. Frankly, I can't recall what originally fostered the dream of driving truck (I know that "driving truck" sounds like a grammatical error, but it is how those of us who drive trucks refer to the process of doing so).

It may have been stories my dad told our family about cross-country trips he made periodically with his cousin, Dick, in Uncle Dick's eighteen-wheeler. It may have been enhanced by the short-lived but enthralling-to-me television series *Cannonball* of the late 1950s. It was patterned on the wonders and travails of a team of long-haul truck drivers' adventures with saving runaway trucks, preventing hijacking of loads, and such.

Or it may have been my own experiences riding in the cabs of semis that stopped to pick me up as a hitchhiker traveling to and from both Wenatchee Valley College and Washington State University when other rides home or to school weren't available. Whatever the reason, driving truck has long been a dream of mine. Twenty-five years ago, in fact, my wife, Mary Jane, gave me a truck-driving lesson at the United States truck-driving school in Commerce City, Colorado, to sate my already full-blown dream at that time.

Mary Jane and our three daughters all joined me at the training facility to watch my lesson. In fact, the three girls, ages seventeen, thirteen, and eight at the time, joined the instructor and me for some of the very rudimentary driving—back and forth—in the lot. It was clearly one of my favorite birthday gifts of all time.

My career in higher education public policy, however, continued to blossom, so truck driving was placed on hold.

Prior to retiring, I had already begun to plan for the transition. This initially began by exploring various training opportunities. In doing so, I shared my dream with colleagues who might know which colleges or other institutions had the best training programs. I included colleagues at the Colorado Department of Higher Education, of which I had at one time in the last century been the executive director, and my friend Leah Bornstein, president of Aims Community College, which has a CDL training program. When encouraged by friends and colleagues to consider consulting in the field from which I was retiring, I also told them of my truck-driving interest—and told them that if I wanted to continue the work I had been doing, I wouldn't be retiring.

Ergo, word got around that I *said* I was going to retire to become a truck driver. And this really seemed to tickle the fancy of a lot of folks. It was included in introductions of me when I was presenting at state and national meetings and conventions, it was a topic of conversation at receptions, and it led to the receipt of a number of related gifts—toy trucks, trucker T-shirts, numerous trucker hats, belt buckles, and so on. It got to the point where I almost had to do it, even if I had not been so excited to do so, because expectations were high.

CHAPTER 2
PREPARING TO BE A TRUCK DRIVER

AFTER EXAMINING THE options, I decided to enroll in the CDL training program at Aims Community College in Greeley, Colorado. Aims CC made a lot of sense because Greeley is only about fifty miles from Lafayette, where I live. And I could easily drive on a daily basis.

As a higher education professional that portends to know the ropes, I was a bit chagrined when I actually screwed up and missed the deadline for enrolling in the desired course. I prefer to consider it a misunderstanding, of course, but others may be correct in asserting that I simply screwed up. I had contacted Aims CC in late June, shortly after retiring, to express my interest in enrolling in its program. They had given me the time and indicated that there was still room in any of the programs at the college (the college begins a new program every four weeks or so). I indicated I would be most interested in the program beginning in mid- to late August.

With that accomplished, I proceeded with a rather hectic postretirement life, which included the wedding of my youngest daughter, a two-week vacation with friends at our vacation home on Lake Chelan in North Central Washington, and then a leisurely trip home to Lafayette, Colorado. Upon arriving home, it was time for me to get ready for my truck-driving course.

I called Aims CC to let them know I was ready to go. They informed me not only that I wouldn't be able to get in the course beginning in August because it was full, with a class of three students already paid and enrolled, but before I could enroll, I had to secure a CDL permit (not a license, just a permit) from the Colorado DMV and a US Department of Transportation (DOT) medical certification that I was medically fit to drive a truck.

I immediately got on the task and hoped for a miracle—that one of the three students would drop out or something. I know, I know, that was a terrible thing to hope for, but I did. My bad.

I visited the DMV office in Boulder, Colorado, of which Lafayette is essentially a suburb, to get the skinny on what I had to do. To get the CDL permit, I would have to pass three separate written tests—a general truck-driving knowledge test, an air brakes test, and a combination vehicle test. The best way to prepare was to study the Colorado CDL Manual. Unfortunately, they were out of written copies but told me I could find it online.

So, home I went to begin reviewing the manual. I was totally blown away with what I found. It was a 135-page document filled with rules, requirements, and lessons of the road. There was a section on the parts of the tractor, that's the cab and engine, and the trailer. It included hints, warnings, and a hefty focus on safety on the road and in preparation for being on the road. All in thirteen chapters.

My initial thought was that I would knock this out in a couple of days. However, the detailed nature of each chapter—or section, as the manual called them—required much more attention than I had anticipated, in part because I was a true novice at understanding trucks and driving them. As a result, I worked on one chapter per day and was able to complete the review of the manual in about ten days. During this time, I continued to be in touch with the folks at Aims CC. I indicated I anticipated I would have my CDL permit and DOT medical certification before the beginning of the August course, should a spot open up. Their response was "Yeah, yeah, we know."

Wednesday before the beginning of the course, I drove to a TA truck stop on the west side of Denver, about thirty miles away, where there is a medical service that provides the exam for the DOT medical certification. I received that certification. The next day, I went to the DMV to take the three written exams required to receive the CDL permit. I arrived just after lunch to find the DMV overwhelmed, both because the previous day its computers had gone down, leaving a backlog from that day, and because the University of Colorado, which is located in Boulder, was just coming back into session, and there were hordes of students from out of state seeking Colorado driving licenses.

But I was resolute. I stuck it out, and finally I was invited to begin my testing around 4:00 p.m. I passed each of the tests with relative ease, though I must admit that I did not ace them. Thank God for the manual; I would not have done nearly as well had I not spent the time I did in preparation. It turns out driving a truck safely and responsibly is not as intuitive as many may believe it is.

With permit and medical certification in hand, I let the folks at Aims know that I was ready and raring to go. And lo and behold, they indicated that there was a *chance* that I might be able to start the following Monday. My terrible hoped-for miracle may have been becoming true.

One of the enrolled students did not realize that he had to have the permit and medical certification before starting the course and thus probably wasn't going to be ready to go on Monday—so I should "stand by." Rather than stand by, I took a chance and drove to Greeley Monday morning and called the instructor about a half hour before the course was to begin.

He invited me to come by, letting me know that he was not keen on trying to fit four people into the course because it reduced the amount of individual attention that each received, and that I might get bumped if the third person was able to get his required documents within the first couple of days. I indicated that I appreciated the opportunity and would understand if I got bumped to a later date.

CHAPTER 3
TRAINING TO DRIVE TRUCK

SO BEGAN MY truck-driving training. The initial phase involved the precheck. Similar to what aircraft pilots do before every flight, truck drivers are supposed to do a similar precheck of the combination tractor and trailer before every trip. Truth be told, this doesn't always happen, but to pass the CDL exam, you must conduct a comprehensive examination of 181 items on the tractor and trailer. You must be able to identify the item, check that it is neither cracked nor broken (or has no abrasions, bulges, or cuts if it is rubber rather than metal or plastic), and check that it is securely mounted and has all hardware in place. In addition, you must indicate whether there are any leaks if it is an item that could leak (like brake lines or radiator hoses). On many items, you must assure that they are clear of debris, and other items have unique, idiosyncratic, required examination, such as checking the tread depth on tires (which can legally vary depending upon whether the tires are on the front of the tractor or not), paying attention to the slack in belts and each brake's slack adjuster (all have different but quite specific allowances), and assuring there are no illegal welds on wheels.

By the way, the precheck had to be performed without any notes. On the first day of class, learning each of these 181 assigned tasks seemed like a mighty daunting assignment. I must say, however, that I was quite taken by the names of a number of these different parts. My favorites include the *glad hands,* which connect the air brake lines from the tractor to the trailer, the *slack adjusters,* which connect the brake push rod to the brake cam and allow for slight tolerances of slack in braking, the entire tractor/trailer coupling system (including the *apron, fifth wheel, sliding fifth wheel platform and assembly, kingpin, and jaws),* and the *splitter,* which simply splits the gear shifter between the lower five to eight gears and the upper five to eight gears, depending on the transmission that the tractor has. My training was on a ten-speed transmission. As intimidating as learning the function and examining each of these parts seemed on day one, by the end of the first week, all four of us in the class had mastered the task, proving in my case that you can, indeed, teach an old dog new tricks.

You will note that I just mentioned "all four of us." As it turned out, the person who had not been able to begin on the first day of class, for lack of a CDL permit and medical certification, was able to get those fairly quickly and arrived for class on the third day. As noted earlier, this development meant that I might have to drop out and await the next class. Fortunately, however, our instructor, Glen, had apparently become comfortable with our group and allowed me to stay. I truly appreciated his doing so but also realized that my remaining meant that each of my three classmates would be receiving about 25 percent less time and attention, at least on individualized training activities, and I felt a bit guilty about that. Obviously, though, not guilty enough to self-select out of the class.

In the end, I was not only glad to have been allowed to stay, because I was able to complete my training earlier, but also because I came to thoroughly enjoy my classmates. They were an eclectic group, wholly different from the colleagues I had worked with throughout my career in higher education. Matt was the natural leader of the group. He had been a parole officer for the state of Colorado, had tired of that, and was following his brother, who was doing quite well with a small independent trucking company. Alan, a strikingly handsome Hispanic man, had been working in a manufacturing plant, but the noise in the plant was causing him to lose hearing, so he needed to find a new job. His dad was an independent trucker, so trucking was a logical alternative. And Chris, the person who had missed the first couple of days of class, had recently been laid off from an oil and gas industry firm due to the reduction in oil and gas extraction in Colorado and wanted to get his CDL-Class A license simply because it would allow him to be rehired at a higher salary; he really had no desire or intent to become a regular truck driver. These guys were all in their midthirties or forties and looking for new careers. And they were smart. I don't know if they are typical of most truck drivers—I'll learn that over time—but though they may not have had doctorates from Stanford as I do, they were clearly as intelligent as I, and in many respects, more so. Not only that, they were just damn nice. To some extent, I was degrading their training by staying in the class, yet they were continuously supportive of me as I struggled, just as they did, to gain the knowledge and skills required to be a truck driver. Our opinions differed on a variety of issues—gun control, federal environmental regulations, presidential candidates, and more—but our discussions of these were thoughtful, reasonably respectful, and often tinged with a bit of humor.

After learning the precheck, next up was driving. And the first part of this was learning what is referred to as the *skills* component of driving. It might more appropriately be called *backing the damn truck*, and it is without doubt the most difficult part of learning to drive a truck. For purposes of preparing for the CDL exam, this skills training involves learning (or attempting to do so) four specific backing exercises. The first is simply learning to back the tractor and trailer in a straight line. That may sound simple, but I can assure you that backing both the trailer and tractor between the cones, at least initially, was no mean trick. Our instructor, Glen, provided what turned out to be superb advice: simply keep the trailer in your rearview mirror and turn the steering wheel slightly to the left if the trailer heads a bit to the right and disappears, or vice versa, adjust slightly to the right if the trailer moves left. Easier said than done, though. In my case, I initially was prone to three errors. First, I had a hard time adjusting to the "left to turn right, right to turn left" element because it was so different from simply backing a car. I had backed boat and orchard trailers in the past, but they were short enough to allow a quick recovery. Not so with a forty-foot trailer. Second, I was overcorrecting. In part, that was because the total disappearance of the trailer when it started moving to the right was quite intimidating, creating a strong incentive to radically correct, and you shouldn't do anything radical in backing a truck. In part, though, the overcorrecting was simply a function of not having developed the feel for modestly adjusting the steering. Third, I was initially behind the curve; in backing a truck, you have to anticipate the effect of steering. This means that you must make the modest steering adjustment as quickly as possible when the misalignment appears but also that you hold the adjustment slightly longer than might seem necessary because it takes the trailer a bit of time to respond.

It's not just about the trailer though. You also have to get the tractor straightly aligned and, thus, between the cones. Virtually all four of us had as much problem with this as with getting the trailer aligned. It's not that this task is so difficult, but rather because it's just easy to forget that as the trailer goes one direction, the tractor, just like your car, is going the opposite direction, and in the end, they both have to be aligned.

Just as with the precheck, though, by the second day, all four of us had the straight backing down pretty well. I must confess that I was perhaps the least proficient in this, but I was able to get the exercise done with no more than the allowable one pull-up and one *stop-and-check.*

Second up in the skills event was learning the cross-over backing exercise, which included learning both the cross-over from left to right and from right to left. Ouch! When you back a truck with a turn involved, you entirely lose sight of what you are doing because you either lose sight of the trailer or the trailer blocks sight of what you are doing. As a result, you simply have to learn how to get the truck and trailer turned blind. Now, again, Glen provided great instruction, and it was quite similar to what videos we had watched suggested; you just turn as sharply as possible, back for three seconds, then turn sharply the other direction for three seconds, by which time you should be able to see the rear wheels of the trailer and the cones and begin to adjust your steering to get into the desired space between the cones. Yeah, right. First, one person's three-second count can vary quite a bit from another's, but the truck doesn't know that. Second, at least in my case, the truck might be bucking because you have inadvertently (or perhaps subconsciously advertently) kept your foot on the brake rather than just letting the idling engine do its work in backing the truck. Third, remembering where the rear wheels need to be and bringing the tractor around into alignment is multitasking that truly tests a novice driver. Fortunately, on this training exercise, you are allowed *two pull-ups and two stop-and-checks*. And as difficult as learning this task is, all four of us mastered it, though I do remember one of my efforts early on that took thirteen pull-ups to get the trailer between the cones.

These first two skills—straight backing and cross-over backing—are both on the final test for the CDL, so they must be mastered.

Next up was to learn to parallel park, again from both the left and right. I've always been proud of my automobile parallel parking prowess, so I was sure I would be good at this skill. After all, it seemed to me that this was simply a variant on cross-over parking, which I had already mastered—well, maybe not mastered but that I could do tolerably. Just as with cross-over parking, we were allowed two *pull-ups* and two *stop-and-checks*. Alas, however, it was not just a simple version of cross-over parking but an even more complicated skill, less due to getting the trailer into position than in bringing the tractor into the parking space without either clipping the cones in front or backing over the curb. So, getting the truck parallel parked required more finesse than had either of the previous skills. All four of us in the class, more or less, accomplished this skill, though seldom within the two allowable pull-ups, which meant we would likely be getting demerit points on this exercise in the final test.

Finally, the fourth skill was the alley park, which requires you to pull in perpendicular to an alley and back the trailer ninety degrees into a parking spot. This skill both looks and is by far the most difficult. Furthermore, though I didn't realize it at the time, this type of backing is frequently required on the road, for example, when you are parking between trucks in a truck stop or backing into a loading ramp between trucks at a terminal. Similar to each of the other three skills, though, Glen guided us through the exercise, and after much practice, sweat, and stress, we figured out how to do this. Again, none of us often achieved this parking within the two allowable pull-ups, but we got through it.

So, despite what seemed like a daunting set of tasks, after about a week of practice, we all had the skills components down, more or less. The good news is that the scoring on the CDL test provides some leeway in demonstrating competency in these skills. I have already mentioned the pull-ups and stop-and-checks allowed for each. On the final test, you are also allowed to receive up to twelve demerit points and still pass the test. Given we were all pretty confident that we could perform the straight backing and cross-over backing without any demerits, that left us with twelve points likely available for the rest of the test, and fortunately, the rest of the test includes either parallel parking or alley parking, not both. Furthermore, you accumulate only ten points on any single exercise that you attempt but cannot execute. As a result, we all should have been able to pass the test without amassing the thirteen points that would signify a failure.

So, it was on to the third and final portion of our training—the road test. This was what I had been waiting for—driving truck. The precheck had been informative, and the skills development had been valuable learning, but driving the truck was why I was in this class. At first, the four of us shared time with Glen as our passenger/mentor, driving around a large parking lot at the rodeo grounds in Greeley, Colorado. Initially, we practiced double clutch shifting and gradual braking. That is opposed to grinding gears while shifting and jerking braking, which is where we started. Once we had these two skills more or less in hand, we practiced double clutch downshifting. Now, the physics were just the opposite. Instead of upshifting into a gear where the new gear would operate at lower RPMs (revolutions per minute), in downshifting, you were moving into a gear that would be operating at slightly higher RPMs, so it was a quite different exercise. All was manageable, however, and within a couple of days, we were ready for the road. That was the good news. The bad news was that we all no longer needed to be there the entire day and scheduled times when we would drive, which meant we would no longer be sharing time together. I had grown quite fond of my three classmates and would miss their camaraderie.

The driving itself, however, was every bit as enjoyable as I imagined it would be. It, too, however, was not a piece of cake. In a truck, you want to stop well behind the stop sign or vehicle in front of you. The general rule is that you stop while you can still see the rear wheels of the vehicle in front of you. That's much farther back than I typically stop, so it took some adjustment. You are also expected to check your mirrors every few seconds. Initially, I thought that was both unwarranted and difficult to remember. It turned out to be both routine and helpful, because you're looking in your mirrors not only to monitor traffic behind you but also to assure that the truck and trailer are in the lane, which is most easily assessed by looking at alignment of the trailer in the mirror. I could discuss myriad other aspects of the driving lessons, but suffice it to say that I learned a great deal and enjoyed it very much. It helped that I had a great instructor, who had both patience and a decent sense of humor.

Taking the CDL Exams

I completed the driver's training course on Friday, September 16, and was scheduled for the CDL exams to begin at seven o'clock Saturday morning, September 17. That meant an early wake-up for me, given the fifty-minute drive from Lafayette to Greeley and the expectation relayed by my instructor, Glen, that "it would be appreciated" by the examiner if I arrived a bit early to help set up the cones on the course. So, I was up at 5:00 a.m. and out of the house at 5:45, still a bit tired but also a bit anxious. The first of the three exams was the precheck, and I wasn't too concerned about passing that portion. I had the parts down pretty well, and you were allowed to accumulate up to thirty demerit points out of a total of one hundred on this section. As expected, I did well on this, with the examiner, Mike, indicating I had aced this section.

Next came the skills portion, and frankly, I was a bit nervous because I was anything but the star of the class on backing the truck. The first exercise was backing straight, and that went quite well, with no demerit points being assessed. Then came the cross-over backing exercise. Fortunately, I was assigned the cross-over from left to right, which I felt more comfortable with than the right to left. Still, I had not exactly mastered this exercise, so I was a bit anxious. But damned if I didn't nail it. Well, not exactly nail it—that would presume backing in without any pull-ups. But I did get the tractor and trailer between the cones with only one of the two allowed pull-ups, and I probably could have backed it in without the pull-up had I been a bit more bold, which of course would have been stupid in the exam because I might also have blown it and accumulated demerits.

So, two down with no demerit points and only one exercise left, leaving twelve safe demerit points available for the final exercise. Mike had selected parallel parking with the curb on the left for this exercise. From my perspective, that was much better than parking with the curb on the right, because having the curb on the left provides much better visibility of the trailer, and it sure was a lot better than having to take a shot at an alley park. Still, parallel parking was going to be a lot tougher than the first two exercises. I got the truck aligned and ready for the exercise, and off we went; three seconds turn of the steering wheel to the right to bring the trailer left into the parking space, bringing the tractor back in line with the trailer, and wow, the truck was moving more comfortably into the space than it had ever done for me before.

Just to check, though, I decided to take one of the two allowable stop-and-checks. I wanted to make sure that the trailer was coming around as nicely as it looked like from the cab and that the tractor was in good stead as well. So, I stopped, put the transmission in neutral, and set the parking brake, as required, then stepped out of the cab (keeping contact with at least three surfaces at all times, as required). I began my inspection, and, indeed, it was good. As I was preparing to reenter the cab to prove my newfound prowess as a driver, though, Mike looked at me and reminded me that when I was finished, I just had to honk the horn. This hint brought me back to reality. If I simply entered the cab and signaled that I had tried but was done, I would receive ten demerit points and complete the skills examination successfully. On the other hand, if I continued on, who knows what might happen. So, I pulled the country air horn and declared victory.

Finally, it was time for stage three—the road test. This was both the most fun and potentially the most risky. Although you were allowed a number of demerits on this test and could still pass, there were certain mistakes that caused automatic failures, including driving over a curb, failing to get into gear in an intersection, having an at-fault accident, driving dangerously, and so on. I actually was feeling reasonably comfortable with driving, but I was far from flawless and knew how easy it was to catch a curb or miss a gear.

This test begins with a testy start. There is a stop at the edge of the examination lot, before entering the street, and then a sharp left turn out of the lot and an almost immediate stop on an incline at the end of a short block. So, you're already a bit harried about having had to make two stops, a sharp turn without cutting the turn short and bringing the trailer into the approaching lane of traffic, then stopping again and facing a start on an incline from that stop. Yikes. But we had practiced this enough that it went well. Two turns and two blocks later, though, Mike said to take a left. Now, up to this point, we had always taken a right turn in class. Clearly, we were now taking a route I had never seen before, and my lack of knowledge of the byways and highways of Greeley instilled a good bit of anxiety, but off we went. We returned to the truck yard at 9:15, two and a quarter hours after beginning, Mike provided me with the form indicating I had passed the tests required to receive a commercial driver's license. First thing Monday morning, I was at the Colorado Department of Motor Vehicles to pick up my CDL Class A license. I had made it.

CHAPTER 4
I'M A TRUCK DRIVER;
NOW TO FIND A RIDE

WHILE I WAS certainly pleased to have secured my CDL, now I needed to go out and get a job. And it had been a mighty long time since I had been on the job market. I had been recruited for virtually every job that I had held since 1977, almost forty years. Sure, I had occasionally applied for a job, but those were applications based on a dream, not a necessity. So, frankly, I wasn't exactly sure how to go about searching for a job. Before jumping into a job search, I needed to settle on just what kind of job I wanted and then prepare for the search.

One of the first things I did was try to get the lay of the land, so to speak. I had seen the job reports indicating that truck drivers were in great demand; with the number of jobs available greatly exceeding the number of candidates for those jobs, or as I would have said in my previous professional life, this was an occupation where demand greatly exceeded supply. I presumed, therefore, that the world was my oyster because I was part of the precious dearth in supply. What I soon learned, however, was the dearth in supply was for experienced drivers looking for a long-term career. Job listings called for at least six months' experience, more often a year, and sometimes as much as three years of experience. I had a total of about 150 miles, accumulated during my recent training.

This didn't concern me too much, though, because I was already thinking about pursuing a rather nontraditional truck-driving career. Given I had a generous retirement package, I really didn't need to make a lot of money, and because my wife and I also wanted to travel and enjoy life, I also wasn't crazy about working full-time/full-year. Therefore, I envisioned searching for a limited number of arrangements with firms that had an occasional need for a substitute or itinerant driver. To pursue this, I needed to establish a business from which to seek such possible positions, perhaps as an employee but also possibly as a contracted driver. I came up with what I thought was a clever, if not cute, name for my operation—D Livery. I ordered a small number of business cards and applied through legalzoom to establish my new business as a limited liability corporation (LLC). Most of my family and closest friends wanted me to include "cowboy" somehow in the name of my company, because that is the name my grandsons have given me as my grandpa name, but I was a bit apprehensive because a number of truck drivers are real cowboys, and they might not be all that pleased with an urban cowboy like me debasing a moniker that they legitimately treasure.

For some years, I had been admiring a beautiful cherry-apple-red Freightliner tractor and elegant white and chrome trailer that frequently were parked along the route I daily drove to work in Boulder. I was intrigued not only with the truck but also with the business it served—servicing and refabricating vintage automobiles. What could be better than driving truck and doing so with a cargo of exotic automobiles! So, my first effort to secure a job was to visit this business. I walked in, found the owner of the business sitting at a desk just inside the door, and introduced myself. I told him I had admired his truck for a number of years, that I had just recently retired and secured my CSL-Class A license, and that I wanted to drive truck for him. He looked at me and said that this was unbelievable, because he had just lost his driver and was about ready to advertise for the position. He indicated that it was not the greatest job in the world because he only needed a driver episodically. I explained that was exactly what I was looking for. And he offered me the job. I had my first gig. Now, it didn't mean I was going to be on the road right away, because he didn't have any immediate need for a long haul and wouldn't for a while. His business specialized in vintage racing cars, and the racing season had just ended and would not begin anew until the following spring. Nonetheless, I was on my way.

The next couple of weeks, I completed a number of applications online, some for more traditional jobs, others more aligned with my desire to work as a substitute or part-time driver, but heard nothing in return. Every day, there were about ten to twenty offers from online job search firms to help me find the perfect job, but none of the jobs they displayed looked like they would like me, nor did I particularly like them. I also visited a few nearby businesses that were advertising for drivers. They were all very pleasant, but none eagerly sought my employment. Apparently, a seventy-year-old rookie didn't fit well in their respective wheelhouses.

I began to wonder if, perhaps, I should become an owner/operator. I had actually started to consider this during my training because driving every day from Lafayette to Greeley and then home again, I would pass rb Ritchie Bros., a business that auctions heavy equipment, including truck tractors and trailers. So, I decided to attend an auction they were conducting on October 13. I showed up early to register and was glad that I had because the registration line was already long when I arrived. Not to worry, though; the truck tractors didn't go on auction until 10:30, and the trailers until a little after noon. The day turned out to be pure enjoyment. When the auction of tractors began, I was totally infatuated. All in all, they auctioned off more than 120 tractors, with selling prices ranging from about $5,000 for a forty-year-old truck to $117,500 for a one-year-old upscale Peterbilt. Of course, auctions are always fun, but this one was also very informative. I went solely to get a feel for what it might cost me to get into a reasonable tractor, and perhaps a trailer as well, and discovered that I probably could afford to do so if I was prepared to shell out somewhere between $25,000 to $40,000.

In late October, however, my inquiries seemed to hit pay dirt. Two well-respected companies—Navajo, a trucking company, and American Furniture Warehouse (AFW), a large company that has its own transportation unit—indicated an interest in me. So, suddenly my problem was that I had two options to consider, rather than the void I had been experiencing. After some telephone conversations, Navajo accepted me into their novice driver's program and scheduled me for their orientation training. AFW called me to indicate that I didn't meet their usual requirements, because of my lack of driving experience, but that they were intrigued by my unusual resume for a truck driver and would like to meet me and see if something might work out. So, I had two live possibilities.

I accepted the invitation to interview with AFW, with the location of the interview being in Westminster, Colorado, about twenty miles from my home. The interview went well, and they indicated that they would accept me into their orientation, with the first stage of that orientation being a driving test to see how much training I would need. After weighing the two options, I decided to go with AFW, basically for two reasons. First, I favored the nature of their loads, which was furniture loaded from the base of the trailer up, over the Navajo cargo, which was often hanging pork and beef. As a novice driver, I wasn't crazy about the prospect of pulling a top-heavy trailer with a swaying cargo. And second, I really liked the folks I had met at AFW and liked the territory that their over-the-road (OTR) trips covered. So, I contacted Navajo, indicating that I was no longer interested in a job with them—in retrospect, a bad decision.

After some understandable delays, I was scheduled for the test drive with AFW and showed up on a Sunday morning for the experience. As had been my experience in the initial interview, my examiner, Julian, was a great guy. I breezed through the precheck, doing extremely well according to Julian. Then it was on to the road test. The tractor was a beautiful red Kenworth T680. It was much nicer than the older Kenworth on which I had trained, but it was also a bit different; it was a thirteen-speed transmission, rather than ten speeds, which meant the gears were differently placed, and it was a sleeper unit, so the tractor and cab were longer than I had previously experienced. No big deal, or so I thought.

Julian instructed me to drive out of the yard, around the facility on the surface road, then back into the yard to the trailer we were to pick up. The trailer was also much nicer than the trailer with which I had trained. It was nearly new, and, more importantly, it was a fifty-three-foot trailer, thirteen feet longer than the trailer with which I had trained. Though I had never actually hitched a trailer to a tractor, I had studied how to do so, and I did just fine in executing this maneuver.

After connecting the trailer to the tractor, we were off. I pulled the trailer out quite nicely and safely from between two other trailers and headed out of the yard onto the highway. The initial turn on to the road wasn't as good as I would have liked, driving slightly over the curb, which no doubt was in part because of my lack of familiarity with the longer trailer. Shortly thereafter, we were headed on to Interstate I-25 toward Denver, with instruction from Julian to get to the left lanes as quickly as possible so we could take an exit on to another interstate—I-76. All of this went reasonably well, though I was clearly struggling with shifting gears, in part because of my lack of familiarity with the shifting pattern with the thirteen-gear transmission. This became a particular issue in the downshifting, which was not going smoothly. But the drive continued reasonably well, from my perspective, though not as well as I would have hoped.

We returned to the yard to perform the skill test of alley parking the trailer between two other trailers. Frankly, I was a bit apprehensive about this exercise because I had performed this in the past only between safety cones, not between actual trailers, and because I was now doing so with a longer trailer than I had ever backed before. Julian indicated that I had thirty minutes to accomplish this task, though it usually took much less than that. My initial pass was nearly disastrous. I had not pulled forward enough to fit the trailer in and nearly hit one of the trailers in backing up. While close to a disaster, I didn't hit anything, just got a bit flustered, and pulled up farther to get a better shot at the parking slot. This time, all went well, and with a couple of stops to get out and check my progress and a couple of pull forwards to straighten things out, both of which are common and acceptable, I completed the alley park and did so in about fifteen minutes. I then dropped the trailer and returned the tractor to its parking space in the yard.

Julian and I then debriefed and signed a few forms. He indicated that I clearly wasn't an experienced driver, that I had not performed up to snuff on some aspects of the drive but had done well on others, which they had expected, given my lack of experience, and that Mike, his supervisor, would be in touch about whether they would take me to the next step or not. This caught me a little off guard, because I thought I was in and that the driving test was simply to demonstrate how much additional training I would need, not whether or not I would be allowed to go forward. I want to make clear I don't believe this was the fault of folks at AFW; rather, it was simply my lack of fully understanding their expectations.

The following day, Mike called me to indicate that they just didn't think that my driving was up to snuff, with particular concern about the close call on the alley park and a couple of other reported close calls on turns where I didn't clear the curbs or came too close to obstacles in the yard. I thought I had recovered from all of those decently, but obviously they did not, so I was bid adieu by AFW. I appreciated that they were willing to consider me, even though they seldom bring on board a driver with as little experience as I had.

I was also humbled by not performing adequately for their consideration. But stuff happens in life, and I got right back online to look at other options. Mike at AFW had suggested that I talk to Swift transportation, because they have a true training program for novice drivers. So, I contacted Swift online, filling out their brief application, and received a call within minutes indicating I had been approved for conditional hiring and asking when would I be available to begin orientation. I indicated that I had a couple of commitments over the coming week and a half, so, if it was okay, I would like to delay beginning until December 12, two weeks hence, and the recruiter said that was fine; she would book me for that time and would be in touch with details at a later date. Subsequently, I also received an email from her indicating the same information.

So, I again had an offer of employment, and I was very appreciative, though this time I was a bit more cautious about whether or not this was the real deal. And, indeed, I began to be a bit concerned when no further contacts from the Swift recruiter followed. So, on the Wednesday before the Monday on which the orientation was to begin, I emailed, then phone messaged her to see what was up. Thursday morning, another recruiter called me to apologize for the lack of attention, indicating that my original recruiter was no longer with the company and that she had not signed me up for the orientation. That was not a problem because there was still room for me; she would take care of getting me everything I needed, and all was well. And, indeed, within fifteen minutes, I received the letter of conditional employment, the instructions for preparing for orientation, and instructions of when and where to meet Monday morning in Denver. This contact did indeed sound more significant, given it also instructed me to pack sufficiently for at least ten days and be prepared for being on the road for up to six weeks. We'll see.

CHAPTER 5
DRIVER'S PURGATORY

ON THE FOLLOWING Monday, I did, indeed, begin my employment with Swift Transportation, the largest trucking company in America, with more than eighteen thousand trucks on the road. I soon discovered, however, that the employment of new drivers for Swift, as it had been with AFW, was a multistage purgatory of sorts, and I was only on the first stage. The first three days of employment were to be devoted to a combination of paperwork and orientation to the company—its philosophy, mission, commitments, and expectations, plus its unique rules of the road, so to speak.

We began Monday morning with eight recruits, four of whom were raw new drivers like me, and four were seasoned drivers who were either transferring from a different trucking company or returning to Swift after discovering that the grass was not always greener on the other side. Virtually the entire morning was spent with the eight of us sharing three computers to fill out myriad forms. At first, I was a bit put off that they were wasting our time by not having enough computers for all of us, but in retrospect, the waiting time gave the eight of us time to begin knowing one another. For me, this turned out to be extremely useful because I, by accident of seating arrangements, spent most of my spare time talking with Ray, an experienced driver from Pueblo, Colorado, who was returning to Swift and who became a font of wisdom for me during the entire orientation.

The big test of the day was the driving test. As initially described to us, this was not an all-or-none test but rather just to determine how much training we would need. We soon learned differently, however, when one of the supposedly experienced drivers was told to pick up his stuff and leave because his driving was not up to snuff. Another of the experienced drivers was told he would have to take a backing course to determine if he could remain in consideration for postorientation employment with Swift. And I didn't do so hot either. My drive, in an eight-speed manual transmission freightliner, went okay but not great, except for the shifting, which didn't go well at all. Upon completing these maneuvers, the tester indicated that "Arizona" would have to determine whether I would continue or not. Somewhat concerned and downhearted, I returned to the orientation, which had finished for the day, pulled my material together, and prepared to leave, not sure whether I would be welcome the next day or not.

Just as I was leaving, however, Brittany, our orientation leader, said that they would like to retest me on an automatic, and they wanted to do so immediately. So, off I went with the same gentleman examining my driving. Driving an automatic made all the difference in the world. Driving a relatively new Kenworth T680 tractor, I did quite well, earning numerous compliments from the examiner, who immediately upon completion indicated I was accepted for the next level of purgatory (no need for relying on Arizona this time).

Tuesday and Wednesday orientation sessions consisted of completing more computer forms and classes on the Swift culture, yard etiquette (yard is the term for the area within a terminal where the trucks are parked), DOT rules and regulations, and company policies and procedures, including how to log hours and miles both on paper and on the electronic Qualcomm system used by many trucking companies to monitor the activities of their drivers. What became clear is that Swift is a proud fifty-year-old company that attempts to create a Swift family culture, as difficult as that is with more than twenty thousand employees.

We novice drivers had been told that we would receive our mentor drivers on Wednesday afternoon, so we were all quite anxious Wednesday morning. Unfortunately, one of the new drivers was told to pack his bags and go home Wednesday morning because he failed Swift's medical test, which is a bit more rigorous than the DOT medical certification process. Unfortunately, he was diabetic, which precluded him from becoming a Swift driver. The rest of us, though, received either a mentor (for the novice drivers) or a truck (for the experienced drivers), and I was assigned to be mentored by Edward Gomez, who was going to arrive in Denver the next morning, Thursday. He would be going on his ten-hour mandatory resting period after a full day of driving, and we would be heading out on our first trip on Thursday evening.

So far, my short stint with Swift had been an absolutely fantastic experience, and did it ever continue to be so. My first time behind the wheel of Ed's 2017 Kenworth T680 was driving out of the Denver Swift Transportation (my new company) terminal just after midnight on December 16, 2017, headed to the Wal-Mart warehouse in Loveland to drop a load of cardboard boxes. This was already a new experience because I had never driven at night, which meant I didn't have my usual cheaters for staying in lane (checking the mirrors to assure that the trailer tires were tracking inside the wide lines). Then there was the blind angle backing into a tight space between two trailers in the Loveland yard—no cones to park between this time; real trailers that don't just fall over when you hit them. For those of you unfamiliar with the term "blind," it refers to backing the trailer to the right, which means you cannot see the trailer as it is moving back, so you can't truly track your progress. All went well, however, so we were off bob-tailing (the term for driving without a trailer) to pick up a load of meat in Greeley, Colorado. Hauling meat obviously requires having a refrigerated trailer, known as a *refer*. I know, I know; this is just one of the trucking terms that has different connotations in other settings. After hooking up (another term with multiple meanings), another first for me, we were off on a trip to Wisconsin. And, to my surprise, the load was not hanging beef but rather huge containers of meat. I'll bet that Navajo trucking uses the same type of containers, so my earlier angst about hauling hanging beef was probably all for naught.

We spent our first evening in Sterling, Colorado, me in the upper bunk, which is actually quite roomy and comfortable. The next morning, we were off early to avoid an incoming storm. Ed led off driving because I was still on my ten-hour mandatory break. We were hoping to avoid an oncoming storm and did so, at least for a while. Unfortunately, or perhaps fortunately for gaining experience, the storm caught up with us in Nebraska just as I was taking the wheel, about four in the afternoon. So, my second day of driving was through snow, drifting because of heavy winds, and ice roads because of lowering temperatures. Fortunately, we had a heavy load, which helps a lot in adverse conditions because the rig holds the road better when it is heavy.

We decided to pull off about ten thirty that night near Kearney, Nebraska, a bit earlier than we had anticipated because we passed two trucks jackknifed in the median of I-80 and four cars off the road as well, and it just seemed wise to call it a night. By this point, I was already quite appreciative of the mentor I had been assigned. First of all, he was a nice guy, clearly focused on helping me through this experience. Second, he was from Alaska and had a lot of winter driving experience, so he was able to provide a lot of valuable advice. Plus, he was an owner/operator with an absolutely pristine and fine tractor (truck).

Day three began with me driving to use up my remaining drive time before going on my ten-hour break. It was cold (about ten degrees), and the roads were still a bit icy, but the wind had died down, so driving was a bit less stressful. That evening we stayed at I-80, Iowa, ostensibly the largest truck stop in American in I-80, Iowa—yup, it's its own town. I had my first truck stop dinner there—a buffet, so it included more than I should have eaten, but then again, it was only the second meal I had had since leaving (I had breakfast at a TA truck stop that morning).

The I-80 truck stop was also where I fueled Ed's truck for the first time. And fueling a semi is appreciably different from fueling an auto. There are essentially four fuel tanks that must be checked and fueled. The tractor has two standard diesel fuel tanks, one on each side of the tractor. On most trucks, including Ed's and the one I would eventually have assigned to me, these were hundred-gallon tanks attached to the tractor's frame below the sleeping compartment of the cab. Some trucks have larger tanks, particularly if the truck is designed to haul extremely heavy or long-distance loads. To fuel these tanks, you pull into a fueling bay at a truck stop, and each tank is fueled at the same time by separated fueling hoses located in the fueling bay on each side of the truck, but connected to one fuel pump on the driver's side of the bay that calculates the amount of diesel loaded and price involved. In addition to these two tanks, on a refrigerated trailer, which is what I almost always drove, there is an additional fifty-gallon diesel fuel tank about a third of the way back on the left side and belly of the trailer that fuels the diesel engine of the refer. And, finally, a fourth fuel tank is filled with diesel exhaust fuel, DEF, which, as its name implies, is an emission-control liquid required for modern diesel engines to reduce their pollution. The DEF solution is 32.5 percent urea and 67.5 percent deionized water (one wonders how this solution was discovered). This fuel does not mix directly with the diesel but is injected into the exhaust system to burn off the natural pollutants of burned diesel. Though truck drivers seldom drive close to empty because they can never know whether they will be held unexpectedly in traffic, at a destination, or running the engine to heat or cool the cab at a truck stop, filling even three-quarter empty tanks can be an expensive proposition. If all four tanks need to be filled, the bill can easily exceed $500, which, in part, explains why truck stops are so eager to treat truck drivers mighty fine when they stop for service and fuel.

The next day, we drove to Oconomowoc, Wisconsin, to drop off the load of meat. We stayed at a nearby Pilot truck stop that evening and drove to our next pickup just outside Milwaukee to catch our next load—milk for McDonald's. To get to this pickup, we had to drive through Milwaukee, and I was at the wheel. It was a very cold morning (-14 degrees), and the storm that had blown through the previous evening had left lousy road conditions. There were at least twenty cars and trucks involved in crashes going through Milwaukee, so it was both slow and anxiety provoking, but we got through without incident, only to arrive at the plant to receive our new load and find that we would have to wait off-lot because the diesel in a number of their trucks had gelled in the cold and none of their bays were available for loading.

I walked inside the gate to observe the efforts to get the stalled trucks running. Obviously, you can't heat a fuel tank, so the process involves removing the engine's fuel filters, emptying the gel and liquid from the fuel filters, filling the fuel filters with a mixture of diesel de-gel and nongelled diesel fuel, reinstalling the fuel filters, and hoping the engine will start. This task is neither enjoyable at fourteen degrees below zero, nor does it happen rapidly. After a couple of hours, the plant finally was able to get their trucks moving, thus freeing up the loading docks, and we were able to get our load on board. We were off to Chicago. That leg was uneventful. We unloaded and headed to upstate Illinois to pick up a heavy load of cheese headed to Oklahoma. We made it to Joplin, Missouri, that afternoon and had a meal at Long John Silver's (my mentor, Ed's, favorite restaurant). Our load wasn't due until the next day, so we stayed the evening in Joplin at another Pilot truck stop.

The next morning, we headed to Oklahoma City and off-loaded our cheese. By the time we unloaded and headed for our next pickup farther north in Oklahoma, it was getting late, and our pickup wasn't until the following morning, so we parked in a casino parking lot. Interestingly, they had quite a large lot for trucks; apparently, truckers like to gamble, though not us. The next morning, we picked up a load of frozen hamburger patties and headed to Arizona.

Up to this point, we had been limited on how far we could go each day because I was driving and Ed was basically mentoring. He felt confident, however, that we were ready to team drive, which meant one of us would drive and the other would rest (the ten-hour breaks I mentioned earlier). I took the first leg, driving across the Texas Panhandle, through Amarillo and on to Albuquerque, where Ed took over and drove on to Phoenix. We arrived in Phoenix and off-loaded in the morning. We wouldn't be picking up our next load until the following morning. This gave me enough time to walk to an urgent care clinic and have some stitches removed from a procedure I had performed on my nose a week before all of this adventure began.

The next morning, we picked up a load headed for Sterling Mountain, Illinois, so back across Arizona, New Mexico, and Texas we went. I began that drive and turned the truck over to Ed just outside Albuquerque. He drove through the night, and for some reason, we were routed over nonfreeway roads, so we ended up in Stratford, Texas, at another Pilot truck stop. Stratford, Texas, is a bit different from Stratford on Avon or even Stratford, Connecticut, for that matter. For those of you who remember the movie *The Last Picture Show*, it could well have been filmed in this town, population 2004, no grocery store other than a Walmart, and one closed restaurant (it was Christmas Eve day when we arrived and late Christmas Day before we left). I walked through the old downtown, in which about half the stores were vacant. By this point, in part because of discussions with Ed, I was beginning to understand a bit better the outcome of the recent election. But that's another story.

So we spent Christmas in Stratford. We spent more time in Stratford than in other stops because we were on a "reset." Once drivers have worked seventy hours in seven days, they must take a thirty-four-hour break called a reset. I was at that point, and Ed was nearing it as well. I only had twenty-four hours left on the reset when we arrived in Stratford (given I had been in the sleeper for ten hours while Ed drove from New Mexico, and that time counted as rest), but that still required a twenty-four-hour layover. I had been excited to go to Illinois because I was born in Sterling, Illinois, so this was sort of a heritage trip, and we were going to get there more than a day ahead of time due to team driving. Then we discovered that Mt. Sterling was nowhere near Sterling, Illinois, so Ed arranged for a T-Call (transfer) outside Kansas City, which allowed us to drop our load early for a day truck to deliver the next day.

I should explain what a day truck is compared to a long-haul truck. Long-haul trucks, like we were driving, seldom enter large cities because their length, at sixty-three feet including a thirteen-foot sleeper tractor and a fifty-foot trailer, is very difficult to maneuver in urban centers. Day cabs, on the other hand, lacking the sleeper, are much easier to maneuver and thus can more easily manage city transport. Often, day cabs also haul shorter forty-foot trailers, which makes them even more manageable in urban environs. Enough already.

After dropping our load, we picked up a load of soap (obviously not requiring refrigeration) for Salt Lake City, and we were off. Ed drove the first leg because I had driven from Stratford and was out of time. He traded with me just out of Cheyenne, and guess what? We were in another blizzard. Light high-profile trucks were prohibited on I-80, but we were a heavy high-profile, so no problem. Yeah, right! The winds were very strong, and I often had to hold the steering wheel about one-eighth to one-quarter turns simply to keep the truck going straight. I felt like I was in a sailboat tacking against the wind. At times, the blowing snow erased the road, and only side markers along the highway gave any clue as to where one should go. It was hairy, to say the least, but again, it was great experience, done with someone who had done it many times before. Going to Salt Lake City was great for Ed because that is home for him, at least to the extent that he has a home. After dropping our trailer, and securing another (referred to as a drop and hook), we drove up to his home, where his sort of estranged wife and daughter live, and we stayed there overnight—he at home, me in the truck (my choice).

During our journey, I had come to know vicariously Ed's family. As already mentioned, Ed was married, never divorced but, according to Ed, now just a very good friend of his wife; not truly a spouse, certainly no longer in a conjugal relationship. Which is not to say that he was celibate by any means. Still good friends with his wife, he supported her financially and continued to enjoy a close relationship with his eighteen-year-old daughter who also lived with his wife near Salt Lake City. He also had a son, now in his midtwenties, who was the original reason for his marriage. His son lived in Juno, Alaska, had two children, one by his wife, lived with his wife's mother and grandmother in a single-wide mobile home, and was unemployed and training to be a mixed martial arts (MMA) fighter. Ed remained close to his son as well, conversing via phone with him virtually every week, often to discuss requests from his son for money. So, while Ed made quite good money as a truck driver, netting over $100,000 per year, these funds were covering not only his living expenses but much of those for his wife and adult children, and a bit on the side to assist a couple of other close female friends.

The evening we stayed at Ed's wife's home, Ed arranged to have dinner with his brother and mother at a nearby restaurant in Ogden, Utah, sans his wife. Ed had talked a good bit about his brother, with whom he was very close and who was finishing up a clinical psychology doctoral program. Ed also was clearly working hard, and it appeared successfully, to reestablish a close relationship with his mother, from whom he had been estranged earlier in his adult life but was enjoying a good relationship now. Fascinated by these family dynamics, I eagerly accepted his invitation to this dinner.

On our way to dinner, Ed warned me that his mother was quite infirm. She was, Ed told me, quite old, not in good health, and debilitated to the extent of requiring a walker. He was quite concerned that she may not live all that much longer, so he relished evenings like the one we were about to have. And, indeed, it was a very enjoyable evening. Ed's brother arrived first and was accompanied by his adult son and his wife. They were all bright, erudite, fun-loving folks. When Ed's mom arrived, she was, indeed, using a walker but immediately left it at the coat check and walked without effort to our table. She was just as sharp, witty, and enjoyable as her sons and grandson were, and it turned out she was five years younger than I am. Apparently, Ed had no idea how old I was, or he might have thought I was about to kick off as well. We all had a wonderful meal and evening, and Ed had an even better one than the rest of us. He had flirted throughout the evening with our waitress and shared with me as we left that she had slipped him her number. Indeed, Ed leads a different life than do I.

The next day, we were off to Twin Falls, Idaho, to pick up a load of Chobani yogurt for LA. How perfect was that? Yogurt for LA, just like the movies. Ed drove through the afternoon and night, and I took over just past Las Vegas. So, I drove through California to near Los Angeles, which included descending my first 6 percent grades on I-10. This also happened to be in an area that had recently burned in those wildfires we hear so much about.

We dropped the trailer of yogurt at the Swift terminal near LA, then picked up an empty trailer and headed north to Bakersfield, California, through a section of I-210 known as the grapevine (my second 6 percent decent experience) for our next load back to Illinois. We spent that evening at a TA truck stop, discovered my new favorite chain restaurant, the Black Bear, had a great steak dinner, and prepared to pick up our load the next afternoon. So ended my first two weeks as an over-the-road truck driver. We had traveled just under six thousand miles and had been in fifteen states.

The gig had been every bit as enjoyable and valuable a learning experience as I had hoped for. I was very appreciative to have had Ed assigned as my mentor. His teaching skills had been great, and his stories quite entertaining. Of course, I felt quite sad about missing Christmas with Mary Jane and my kids, who had come home for Christmas, but I knew that was in the cards when I accepted this gig. I still had at least the next two weeks of training with Ed, after which I anticipated getting back home for a few days before getting my own truck.

But enough of the travel log. While describing the first couple of weeks of my over-the-road driving experience helps give a feel for the unique challenges facing a novice driver, both with respect to the challenges of weather and roads and the demands of the job, more of the same would become boring quite fast. So the rest of this treatise will be more about the different phases of learning to drive a truck and various aspects of truck driving, including the actual driving experience and the culture of the truck-driving community.

CHAPTER 6
FREE AT LAST

MY TIME WITH Ed, my mentor, lasted slightly more than five weeks. Upon its conclusion, I had personally driven more than five thousand miles and had visited twenty-five states. We had endured multiple winter storms beyond those mentioned in the previous chapter, including two in unbelievably thick fog. More importantly, we had become good friends and colleagues. We were supposed to part ways in Salt Lake City on a trip from Everett, Washington, to Illinois, but we were held up by a storm in the Northwest that shut down traffic on all interstates out of Washington for four days. We made it to North Bend, Washington, which is right at the base of Snoqualmie Pass on I-90 through the Cascade Mountains. The bad news was that we arrived in North Bend just about an hour after the pass closed, so we were stuck for the duration, and no one knew how long that would be. The good news was that we arrived soon after the closure occurred, so we were able to get a room in a motel across from the only truck stop (fortunately, a TA station) in the area. Within hours after our arrival, trucks were parked for miles along the side of the interstate; we at least had a nice motel room to stay in and access to the TA's Country Pride Restaurant.

This delay, however, was placing in jeopardy my transition to independent driver status, so after a day and a half, I bid adieu to Ed, took Uber to Sea-Tac Airport, and flew on my dime to Salt Lake City to take the exam and backing course required for transition to full-blown driver status. I passed those requirements and was declared a fully authenticated professional truck driver for Swift Transportation Company. There is always a brief transition from student to driver status, so I immediately caught a Friday-afternoon flight from Salt Lake City home to Lafayette, Colorado, via Denver and made arrangements to pick up my truck at the Denver Swift terminal the following Wednesday, giving me my first four days off since beginning driving six weeks earlier.

It was quite exciting to pick up my truck the next Wednesday. I was assigned a 2016 Freightliner with 160,000 miles on it and some modest damage on one fender, probably resulting from hitting a deer. Other than that, the truck was in great shape, and it was mine. The Freightliner Cascadia is a nice truck with a comfortable sleeper unit, including two bunks, a small refrigerator, good storage capacity, and a nice heater. It turned out to be a quite comfortable home for the next three months. It certainly wasn't as grand as the ride in Ed's Kenworth had been; Ed had all of the amenities of the Freightliner, plus a microwave, television, CB (citizens band radio), and Sirius XM radio. Plus, his was a lofty Kenworth, and mine was just a regular Freightliner; in the trucking world, two brands—Kenworth and Peterbilt—are considered the elite trucks, and Freightliners, Volvos, Internationals, and others are "the rest." This also meant I had to place my favorite KW hat in moth balls, because it was considered déclassé to wear a hat of a truck brand other than the one you were actually driving.

But now I was driving my own truck. That was what it was all about. While I assumed this meant I was finally out of purgatory, I soon realized that such was not the case.

When you work for a trucking company, particularly a nonunion company, you are really never out of purgatory. And although many folks think most truck drivers belong to the Teamsters Union and thus are tough guys, such is no longer the case, if it ever was. Most companies, like Swift, are headquartered in right-to-work states so that they can be nonunion companies. Swift made it clear in all of its communications that it was an at-will employer, meaning the company could dismiss a driver at any time they wished. Yes, the dismissal had to be for cause, but cause was broadly defined.

Having come from a union-friendly background, I was initially a bit leery of Swift's nonunion stance, though my overall experience was that the company was quite fair to its drivers. Furthermore, I couldn't feel too uncomfortable with my status because in my forty-five years of service in the public sector, I was, for all practical purposes, always an at-will employee, never having more than a one-year contract. At Swift, and I expect at all trucking companies, all drivers work with a driver leader who is their direct supervisor and supports their driver's success. I was very fortunate to have Ed's driver leader, Jimmy Christianson, ask to have me in his stable of drivers, and he turned out to be a very good leader for me. He kept me busy on the road, provided support throughout my brief tenure with Swift, and was very patient with his new driver.

Driving a truck over the road is not hard work, but neither is it an easy job, and it is certainly full-time to say the least. In the five months I drove for Swift, I had six days off. Now, there were other days when I wasn't driving because I was on the mandatory thirty-four-hour reset required if you accumulate eighty hours on duty in seven days, but those layovers were at truck stops and in my book hardly count as days off. As a company driver, one doesn't arrange her or his own trips; rather, this is done by trip planners working with the driver leader rather than with the driver her or himself. These trip planners have access to your electronic driving logs, so they know how many hours you have available to drive and work to match the time required for possible trips with your available hours. Then they assign you a trip. The driver is not required to accept a prospective trip, but you better have a good excuse for not doing so.

I, like most drivers, preferred long trips because it meant fewer pickups and deliveries, both of which take time and reduce mileage, and time and mileage are critical because drivers are paid by the mile. Once I accepted a trip, it was my responsibility to get to the shipper at the designated time and with a clean trailer. Often, though not always, there was an actual appointment time for picking up the load, and missing that appointment time could mean actually having to reschedule another appointment, which could be a day or two later, or at the very least would mean a delay in loading, often a substantial delay, all of which costs time and money. Delays in loading also create a possible dilemma because they mean you have less time remaining on the clock to reach the receiving destination, which also has a prescribed time for delivery. And arriving late could not only lead to unloading with the same types of delays that could be experienced when loading late but could also lead to financial penalties for Swift, so there was a very strong expectation from the company that you deliver on time. The only exception was for delays caused by inclement weather or mechanical problems.

I should qualify my earlier statement that "driving a truck over the road is not hard work." By this, I meant that it is not strenuous work, at least for most truck drivers. If, by chance, you have read the really good book *Long Haul*, by Finn Murphy, you know about the rigorous job he had driving a moving van. That, however, is a fairly unique niche within the long-haul driving world. Most drivers don't actually load or unload their trucks. That task is left to folks called lumpers who either work for the shipping or receiving company or who contract with those companies to load and unload. Even their job, however, isn't as strenuous as Finn Murphy's was because they almost always load pallets onto the truck with a forklift. As mentioned earlier, I was driving a refer (a refrigerated trailer), which meant I was generally hauling food stuffs, often meat. Had I been responsible for loading this cargo, my job also would have been very strenuous, but I never actually loaded the trailer.

Interestingly, although I didn't load the truck, I was responsible for the load. And, indeed, lumpers varied considerably in their loading and unloading skills. How the cargo is loaded obviously affects the weight distribution in the trailer. By law, and for good reason, the load must be distributed roughly equally over the two axles supporting the trailer (the rear axle of the tractor and the movable rear tandem axle of the trailer). If the cargo is not loaded correctly, the load will not scale correctly, and the driver, not the lumpers who loaded the trailer, will be held responsible. This can result in a substantial fine and citation at a weigh station. Therefore, the driver must weigh each load as soon as possible after loading, and hopefully before passing a weigh station.

Usually weighing the load is done for a modest fee at a nearby truck stop, most of which are equipped with a commercial *CAT Scale* (certified automated truck scale), which means it has been blessed by the DOT. If the load is not balanced, the driver must move the trailer's rear tandem axle back or forward, depending on the maldistribution of weight, until the load is balanced. Usually, this isn't too tedious a task, just a time-consuming one. Moving the axle one notch (about two inches) redistributes the weight by about five hundred pounds. Early in my driving experience, it often took me more (sometimes quite a few times more) than the *first weigh* to get the weight balanced.

Despite this task not usually being too difficult, two factors can make it rather tough to accomplish. First, occasionally the pins holding the axle in place freeze up, making it nearly if not actually impossible to get the lever that releases the pins to actually retract the pins. Obviously, if you can't release the pins, you can't move the axle, and if you can't move the axle, you can't balance the load. This is a particular problem in cold weather but can occur at any time because of expansion and contraction of the steel axle and pins. On one occasion, in Dodge City, Kansas, at a Cargill meat plant, I had to get a tow truck to come to the plant to help me dislodge the pins, and he was able to do so only by lifting the back of the trailer to release the pressure on the axle, allowing me to move the axle to the right position. Also, many shippers and receivers require that the axles be moved to the position farthest back on the truck when loading or unloading because this provides a more stable platform for the forklifts as they work inside the trailer. This means, of course, that even if the lumper balances the load well, the driver often will have to move the axle forward upon being loaded or unloaded.

The second factor sometimes confounding the movement of the rear axle is that a number of states require that the two axles supporting the load (those being the rear axle on the tractor and the axle at the rear of the trailer) be either no more than a certain distance apart or at least a certain distance apart. Most significant in this regard is California, which requires that the rear wheels on the rear tandem axle are no more than forty-three feet behind the kingpin in the fifth wheel assembly. The dilemma with regard to this is that a fully loaded trailer, with forty thousand pounds of cargo, can be difficult to balance at the forty-three-foot mark, particularly if the cargo is not appropriately loaded.

If the load simply can't be adequately balanced by moving the rear tandem axle, the driver does have one additional option, which is to actually move the fifth wheel assembly, which on most tractors is also movable. This is a last-ditch solution, however, because it is harder to do, except on trucks where it is automated. And, of course, on a refer, you can only bring the fifth wheel assembly forward so far because the refer engine, which is affixed to the front of the trailer, needs clearance room when turning the truck.

I soon discovered that driving alone was quite different from driving under the tutelage of my mentor driver. For one thing, driving alone meant there was no one except me to talk to. Though I actually wasn't bad company to myself, I was not nearly as enjoyable to converse with as Ed had been. More importantly, I discovered that there was still a lot I didn't know as well as I thought I did, because Ed had always been there to do the task, assist, or cover for me. A major area in this regard were the "macros" required by Swift to send messages to the company, keeping them apprised of what was going on. Macros are like email messages and are transmitted electronically via the online Qualcomm system available in every Swift truck, and I suspect in most trucks, at least those operating within a trucking company system. There are macros for just about anything you can imagine—precheck, postcheck, refrigerated temperature checks, notice of arrival at a shipper, notice of when you are loaded and departing the shipper, notice of when you have arrived at your destination, notice of when you are unloaded (empty), notice of accident or mechanical problems, and on and on and on. Some of these are mandatory, some voluntary. Some are for the company, and some for the driver. I soon realized that I simply didn't know the macros as well as I should have. Furthermore, I often simply forgot that a macro was required at a certain point. For example, too often, when I arrived at the destination, I was so glad to have arrived and so absorbed with checking in at the shipping/receiving office and beginning the unloading process that I simply forgot to send the *I have arrived* macro, so the company often thought I was running behind even though I was already unloading or loading. Fortunately, Jimmy, my driver leader, was a patient person and helped me negotiate my oft missteps in the world of macros early in my solo driving experience.

I also soon realized that perhaps the toughest aspect of driving was parking and docking the trailer, be that at a truck stop, a shipper, or receiver. Ed had wisely counseled me not to be too proud about parking and to always take the easiest parking spot. At the truck stops and rest stops, the best parking spots are the ones you can drive forward into without any backing maneuver required. To get one of these spots, however, you have to arrive at the truck or rest stop relatively early in the evening. Usually, at least in my case, it was unusual to find such a spot, so most likely I was going to have to back into one of the few available spaces left in the lot, and of course those are going to be the least desirable parking spots in the lot. After a long day of driving, when your mind is a bit numbed, backing into a tight space between two other trucks is no mean trick. Most truck stops have enough space within rows of trucks for a good driver to maneuver her or his backing safely. But a few truck stops, particularly in urban areas where space is precious, and many shippers/receivers have mighty limited space for parking or docking trailers. And it takes a lot of finesse to get into many of these spaces, finesse that is hard to muster up when you are totally whopped at the end of a tough day. I never damaged my or any other trailer in backing up, though I often took quite a long time doing so, often to the consternation of other truckers.

My cautious driving, both in parking/docking circumstances and on the road, was not always appreciated by other truck drivers. In fact, Swift trucks are often the butt of jokes on the CB chatter. In part, this is because Swift is one of the few trucking companies that will hire novice drivers, thus many of us tend to be less expert at the job, be that parking, turning sharply, traversing steep grades, and so on, and our cautious nature is often described in various colorful ways on the CB. Swift is also castigated, however, for driving slowly. This results from the company's decision to govern the speed of its trucks at the lowest level of any major truck carrier, at sixty-two miles per hour maximum speed. Usually this is simply fodder for CB chatter as other trucks travel past you on the highway, but occasionally it leads to quite hostile verbal abuse when traffic conditions mean a Swift truck is holding up faster trucks; given miles mean money, drivers don't like to be held up, particularly by other slow drivers like me.

One advantage I have over most drivers is that I'm driving for the joy of it; I don't have to make a good living at it because I fortunately have a handsome retirement package from my first career. As I prepared for my new career as a truck driver, I told many of my friends that, as a result of my unique circumstances, I was going to drive only when it was safe, sane, and enjoyable to do so. Well, life as a truck driver doesn't quite fit the fairy-tale world I envisioned. You don't get to choose good weather and fair conditions. Within twenty-four hours of driving for Swift, I had driven through snow, sleet, black ice, rain, and heavy winds. The only kinds of bad weather that I have not faced are tornadoes and hurricanes. From my perspective, the worse conditions to drive in are heavy winds (particularly when they are accompanied by blowing snow in a blizzard) or fog. And you don't really have a choice but to drive through these in most circumstances. If the road is not officially closed, you are expected to travel on. In my brief stint with Swift, I often traveled I-80 through Wyoming, which is always windy but often so windy that light-load/high-profile vehicles (that is every empty or lightly loaded semi with a box trailer) were prohibited from proceeding. I remember having to hold the steering wheel as though it were the rudder on a sailboat to keep the truck on the road.

And fog is worse. One evening, traveling west through Wyoming, the fog was so bad that I could only see about fifty feet ahead, following the taillights of the preceding truck. Virtually all car traffic had pulled off, but we truckers had timed destinations to reach, and the road was not closed, so we kept on truckin'. Most of us were driving about forty to forty-five miles per hour, which frankly was too fast for the conditions, but going any slower would have increased the risk of being tail ended. What amazed me, however, was the number of truckers maintaining normal highway speeds and passing us as they raced on. Particularly notable among these fast trucks were the UPS and FedEx trucks, as well as the grain trucks often driven by cowboys who think they are invincible. Most of these trucks apparently made it through, though on almost every trip through Wyoming, I witnessed one or more trucks blown or driven off the road.

Fatigue can factor in as well. I vowed never to drive tired, but it is mighty hard to avoid. While I tried as often as possible not to drive at night, because that was the only time I actually got very tired, it was sometimes simply impossible to avoid. If you are delayed in receiving a load, it may be necessary to drive all night to deliver the load on time. And if you've just been sitting around waiting for a load, the company legitimately expects you to drive when you depart with your load. More common, however, is that you will be expected to deliver in the middle of the night. Many companies prefer that the long-haul trips load and unload in the middle of the night so that they can load and unload their local cargo during the day. So, yes, I did drive when I was sleepy. In fact, I believe that soon self-driving trucks will replace manually driven ones, at least on the over-the-road trips. And I believe the highways will be safer as a result. Robots won't speed, fall asleep, be distracted by whatever, have any difficulty backing their trailer, or give any lip to the clients.

Managing the truck itself was also initially a more significant challenge than I had expected. Early on, I threw a tire chain, which was a bit traumatic. Traveling east near Pendleton, Oregon, one morning, chains were required, and I decided to chain up rather than wait out the storm. This was contrary to the advice my former mentor, Ed, had given me; Ed advised that if the weather is so bad as to require chains, it is too bad to be driving, and you should just pull over and wait for better road conditions. I probably would have taken his advice, but I thought I should at least have some experience putting on chains, and besides, there was a fellow in an old Toyota pickup who was selling his chain-installation services. So, I hired him to instruct me in putting my chains on.

Mission accomplished, I was on my way east on I-40, quite proud of myself. Fifteen miles farther, however, and a half mile from where I was to take my chains off, one of the chains voluntarily shed itself from its tire. I had never thrown a chain, and it really shook me up. I pulled over, picked up the pieces of chain that I had strewn on the highway for a couple hundred yards, removed the remained bits of the destroyed chain, which were wrapped around the axle, and surveyed damage that this episode had created to a small fiberglass panel on the rear of the tractor's cab. Only later would I discover that the thrown chain had punctured one of my tires as well.

Lesson learned; follow Ed's advice whenever possible. Avoid putting chains on, and if you must chain up, drive very slowly (below thirty miles per hour) while driving with chains. I also managed twice to pinch, thus puncturing, the air brake hoses coupling to the trailer. This occurred during very tight turning maneuvers, which will crimp the hoses if they are not installed correctly, and apparently, mine were not. The result is a loss of air pressure and braking capacity. In both cases, I was able to repair the lines with tape to suffice until I could get them repaired.

While driving alone certainly reminded me quickly of how much I didn't know about my new profession, each day brought greater knowledge and experience, and my confidence began to grow. Relatively soon, I was both comfortable and confident that I was now truly a truck driver, that I was not a danger on the road and could become a true asset to Swift Transportation.

As my confidence grew, so did the joy of driving, which was why I had gotten into this business in the first place. And I must tell you that driving a big rig lived up to all of my expectations. I simply love driving truck. Operating the machine itself is a joy. While conducting the precheck each day is a bit tedious, it reminds you of the marvel of this machine and helps you appreciate the privilege you have to be driving the rig. And the driving experience itself is great. Though most of my experience was driving trucks with automatic transmissions, my training was all conducted on trucks with manual transmissions, and my driving since leaving Swift has been almost entirely with manual transmission trucks. While mastering manually shifting a truck, both upshifting and downshifting, takes a while, once you master the task, the shifting of gears actually allows you to essentially commune with your truck, shifting through the gears until you throw the splitter to allow you to the second set of gears. It's just plain fun. Even in an automatic, using the manual option and jake brakes provides a similar experience to be up close and personal with your rig. There isn't anything quite like it.

And the vistas are amazing. One of the very special aspects of over-the-road driving is seeing America. Because you are sitting much higher than in a car, you see much more in your travels. You truly come to appreciate the verse of "God Bless America," "from the mountains, to the prairies, to the oceans white with foam." The Cascades in Washington and Oregon provide the beauty of evergreen-covered mountains. Boulders, rocky outcroppings, and many waterfalls comprise the Rockies in the mountainous west. The many slopes and hollows make up the Appalachians that flow from Pennsylvania through the south. And the Sierra Madres take you from the deserts of the Southwest to the beautiful green valleys of California and then to the teaming humanity of urban Southern California. Then from Southern California, the Sierra Nevadas lead through Tahoe to Nevada and on east. Each of these mountain chains has its unique beauty and grandeur. Each also presents its challenges to a truck driver, with steep grades that challenge the driver trying to maintain speed on the uphill grades and needing to hold speed down on the descent through steep grades.

I used to think the prairies of America were rather boring, especially after hours of traversing them, but I came to really enjoy and appreciate driving through Nebraska, Iowa, eastern Colorado, and Kansas. The space that once bored me became a reminder of the massive space that is America. Most Americans have no understanding of the extensiveness of space in the prairie lands. Traveling through this area of the country helps one understand the importance of both plant and animal agriculture to our country. Such travels also help one better understand and even appreciate why much of the Midwest is so politically conservative, a topic I will cover in more detail later. The sunsets and sunrises remain perhaps my favorite part of traveling through this part of the country. I loved getting up enough before sunrise to drive in the early morn while traffic was light and enjoy the views of farms, cattle, and villages as dawn arrived. Equally enjoyable were the amazing sunsets running across the massive skyline in front of me, particularly as I traveled west.

The oceans are a bit more difficult to enjoy from the cab of a truck, because most highways are well away from the coastline. The coastal areas nonetheless have their own beauty and intrigue, with the West Coast going through wineries, forests, and farmlands, and the East Coast highways flowing through farm lands and orchards as well, but also marshes, deciduous forests, and uniquely southern towns.

As one travels across the country, the towns provide evidence of clearly different local cultures. I was particularly taken by the stark contrast between homes in the Midwest, particularly in Iowa and Minnesota, and those in southern states like Tennessee, Kentucky, southern Ohio, South Carolina, and the Deep South. At least as one travels the interstate highways, the homes in Iowa and Minnesota, though often modest in size, are extremely well kept as well as painted conservatively, mostly in white. In the South, however, homes along the freeway often have substantial clutter, many with numerous autos (working or not), and are often not kept up as well as in the middle of the country. In the west, the communities are much more eclectic, some portions neat and clean, others not so much, and some quite funky.

All in all, though, I consider the opportunity to have seen so much of the country a great gift. Driving a big rig has turned out to be every bit as great as I dreamed it would be.

CHAPTER 7
HERE COME THE DICKHEADS

A NUMBER OF behaviors, of both other truck drivers and of four-wheelers, really aggravate most over-the-road truckers.

The title of this chapter comes from one of these behaviors, the lack of common courtesy. In general, truck drivers are quite a courteous crowd. Other drivers will usually back off in traffic to allow a truck trapped in another lane to merge in front of them. And I can't tell you how many times a driver who was already parked in a truck stop or at a terminal jumped out of the cab to assist me as I was backing in. You will also often note that truckers will signal with flashed lights to indicate when it is safe to pull into their lane after a pass. Without doubt, the standard ethic is to be courteous. I suspect that is why most drivers really dislike those few drivers who think they are more important than any of the rest or who fly off the handle at modest inconveniences.

The title of this chapter is actually a quote from a CB conversation during a traffic backup near Evanston, Wyoming. This occurred while I was still riding with my mentor, Ed. We had been delayed leaving Salt Lake City because of a storm along I-80 through Wyoming but had decided to take a chance on the weather improving and got on the road out of Salt Lake City, Utah, before the freeway had actually reopened in Wyoming. It was a couple of hours from SLC to Wyoming, and we passed into Wyoming, approaching Evanston, which is near the border, about 9:00 a.m. Although the road had ostensibly just opened up for traffic, we soon discovered that a jackknifed truck and trailer had led to another eastbound closure, and we were in a line of trucks running as far in front of us as we could see, and eventually in back of us as well.

As is standard practice, we turned on the CB to get the scoop on what was happening, and it was through the CB that we heard about the jackknifed trailer, with estimates of a two-hour delay. On the CB, the state patrol asked that all truckers get to the right lane to allow emergency vehicles and four-wheelers to move through. Four-wheelers (that would be cars or pickups) were allowed through because they could maneuver around the accident, but there just wasn't room for semis to do so. And for a while, all was copacetic. As time wore on, however, some folks became impatient and broke ranks, and that is what prompted the quote. One person on the CB, noting the approach of some trucks in the left lane, alerted us all, "Here come the dickheads." Ed and I both broke out laughing because it was the absolutely perfect moniker for those jerks.

While such behavior isn't the norm, it is altogether too frequent among truck drivers. Some will pull out to pass on a grade even though they have only a couple of miles per hour more momentum than you have, which leads to them holding up other traffic and denigrating the reputation of all truck drivers. Others will pull in way too early and unsafely after passing you. And clearly some hotheads are simply ill suited to be truck drivers. Many, if not most professional truck drivers, really enjoy driving truck. But that doesn't apply to all drivers. Some are in it because it was the best-paying job they could find. Some are in it because they thought they would love it, but the estrangement from family and community that often accompanies cross-country driving didn't live up to their expectations. And some just don't have the patience to drive truck, because it really requires patience.

Truckers also despise dangerous truck drivers, and unfortunately, there are way too many of those on the road as well. While I understand the rationale for exempting drivers of agricultural trucks from having to secure a commercial driver's license or from abiding by the hour restrictions imposed on other truckers, you don't need to drive very long without realizing how dangerous many of these exempt drivers are. Absent the training required to secure a CDL, many of these folks simply don't know enough about the physics of driving to operate their vehicles safely. And just because it is harvest season doesn't mean a person who has been working too many hours won't be overly fatigued and thus prone to unsafe driving. There are many unsafe drivers, however, who do have a CDL and simply aren't prone to living by the rules of the road. To some extent, this field of work often attracts such individuals who think of themselves as free spirits—by definition, therefore, free of restrictions.

Now, I don't know if this is the case for most truck drivers, but I can tell you that I also got really tired of the CB talkers. The CB radio can be a very valuable tool for a driver, helping to identify potential looming problems ahead or calling for help in an emergency. But too often, at least from my perspective, it is just a way for lonely folks to talk. Regular CB talkers seem to fall into three categories:

- Those who are angry about everything in the world and love to spout the fake news emanating from the alt-right talk show hosts.
- The religious zealots who want to save all of their fellow truck drivers—actually, I should clarify that statement: the evangelical Christian zealots. I never heard a Muslim, Hindu,

Jewish, or Buddhist zealot trying to save my soul. By the way, I'm already a Christian, so I don't need this bullshit.

- The racist, sexist, misogynistic barbarians who believe telling their jokes and preaching their bigotry anonymously over the CB is acceptable behavior.

If you're going to drive truck and use a CB, however, you simply have to be prepared for more exposure to each of these than you might desire, because the nature of the occupation actually fosters such behavior. As an anonymous form of communication, much like the internet, you can say anything and not be held accountable. And for many who spend a lot of time on the CB, it is a way to stay awake when you are tired or simply to talk when you are tired of silence.

Four-wheelers can also be dickheads, though more often than not, their transgressions are borne of ignorance, not arrogance. I personally found three standard behaviors of auto drivers problematic, and from discussions with other truckers, these seem to be pretty pervasive issues. First and foremost, primarily because of the safety concerns, are those four-wheelers who drive in the truck driver's blind spots. Duh: that sign on many trailers that reads "if you can't see me, I can't see you" is so true but apparently an alien idea to many auto drivers. One of the most serious causes of truck/car accidents remains cars that tailgate and then rear-end the truck when it brakes suddenly. Perhaps even more serious are the accidents that occur when a truck turns into a lane that it believes is clear but clips a car that is in the truck's blind spot. This can happen on either side of the truck but most often happens when the auto is on the right of the truck, because the blind spot is more substantial than on the left. And these accidents can be much more serious because, unlike the back of the trailer, there is no guard to prevent the auto from actually going under the side of the trailer, often leading to fatal accidents.

The second auto driver's behavior that really bothers truck drivers is the tendency for four-wheelers to pull into space in front of the truck in heavy traffic. Truck drivers don't leave space between themselves and the vehicle in front as a courtesy to allow naive auto drivers to change lanes. Rather, they leave this space so that they have enough room to stop their eighty-thousand-pound truck if circumstances require them to do so. By crowding into that space, the four-wheeler increases the likelihood that the truck may run right over the top of them in a quick stopping circumstance, and indeed, this is the most frequent and dangerous type of trucking accident. So please, auto drivers, let truckers maintain enough room to drive safely.

The third aggravating behavior of four-wheelers is the common practice of auto drivers passing a truck and then slowing down. I think I understand at least one reason why folks do this; they don't like the view from behind a truck as well as from in front. But if you want to be in front, which is certainly understandable, at least maintain your speed. Remember, truckers get paid by the mile, so when you slow them down, you reduce their salary.

Drivers, be they four-wheelers and other truck drivers, aren't the only folks, though, who drive truckers nuts. The individuals who schedule trips for drivers, be they the trip planners within a trucking company or the brokers who find rides for independent truckers, can be pains in the ass. I'm pretty sure they don't mean to be, but indeed, for two reasons, they often are. First, they serve a master other than the driver; their job is to quickly find a truck to carry the load that the trip planner or broker has promised to have delivered. Their success is based on how much business—that is, how many trips—they can line up, and that means scheduling the drivers as tightly as possible. In principle, this shouldn't present a problem, because most drivers prefer to be on the road; more trips with quicker turnarounds mean more miles for the driver, ergo greater earnings.

Problems arise, however, because the trip planners and brokers, most of whom have never driven a truck, operate on a set of formulas that simply don't reflect the reality of truck driving. For example, at Swift, we were expected to turn a load in one and a half hours. While on paper that seems like a reasonable expectation, it is so only if a door is available to load or unload, if lumpers are available to load or unload, and if product is available in the case of receiving a load. And frankly, seldom are these conditions met, which means loading and unloading often, if not most often, can't be completed in the allotted time. As a result, the driver often uses up more of their on-duty time and may be delayed in either moving on to pick up a new load or in delivering the delayed load, none of which is factored into the trip planner's or broker's expectations. These folks are also notorious for failing to take into consideration traffic and weather conditions. They expect the driver to make the same time in heavy traffic as they would in light traffic. And they expect the driver to make the same time in terrible weather conditions as on a nice sunny day, which is particularly a problem in winter.

Trip planners and brokers are often blamed, however, for conditions well beyond their control, such as the simple absence of loads. Drivers can get stuck for days when trips dry up. As a driver of refrigerated units, it was common for trips not to be available in certain segments of the country simply because harvest had not materialized as expected or food production at a plant had been interrupted for one reason or another.

Another group of folks that can drive truckers nuts are the admitting (loading) and receiving personnel at the customer's facility. Now, let me make it clear that this is not a universal problem. Many of these people were both very competent and very nice. Two problems, however, often arose while loading or unloading. First, sometimes the folks were anything but nice and treated the truckers like dirt. This was more likely in smaller operations, which seemed to employ much less-well-trained personnel. I understand how these individuals can develop attitude. First, circumstances are often out of their control, and they are tired or mad about how the day or night has progressed. And, truth be told, many truckers are pretty disrespectful and demanding of these personnel, particularly when the driver has faced substantial delays or a bit of lip. The second problem with the customer's representatives is that, whether they are nice or not, the processes of loading and unloading trucks are often very disrespectful of drivers. The delays can be very long, most often without any explanation or estimates of time to be involved. Often, I had to wait in a line of drivers just to let them know I had arrived. Even departing with a load often took an interminable amount of time. I experienced this less at well-organized firms like Costco and Cargill, but even companies that pride themselves in efficiency and just-in-time delivery, like AmeriCold and Walmart distribution centers, were notorious for such delays.

All of which is to say that the dickheads come in a variety of characters. Some are just plan jerks, as the reference implies. More, however, are decent folks who are simply ignorant of trucking, whether that is four-wheelers who don't understand the forces of physics involved in driving a truck or planners who presume a truck is a truck and that's it. And some are nice folks working in a business with bad processes that essentially disrespect truck drivers, whether they mean to or not.

Despite these hassles, however, most of the folks who truck drivers deal with are regular folk whose transgressions offset a bit of the joy of driving but not much.

CHAPTER 8
DRIVERS' CUISINE

WHEN I TALK to people about my truck-driving experiences, the first question they invariably ask is about the challenge of backing the truck, but the second usually is about eating on the road. Sometimes, this question about drivers' cuisine is preceded with a nostalgic reference to a stop a person made at a truck stop to eat at a Country Pride or Country Kettle restaurant while on a cross-country car trip. More often, the cuisine question presumes that the trucker's diet is pretty sorry. And, in fact, this chapter will be short because there really isn't much to tell. Back in the day, I am told, most truck stops had some semblance of an in-house managed cafeteria or restaurant to serve their clientele. Not so today. Most truck stops now rely on one or another chain short-order establishment to provide meals, be it McDonald's, Hardies, Subway, Burger King, Wendy's, Arby's, Pizza Hut, or others. Many still have a "hot table," which generally provides fried chicken, pizza, rollups of various types, including various types of hot dogs and sometimes preprepared meals. All in all, it's pretty sorry fare, without doubt, to the ample bellies and heavy Tums or Rolaid usage of many truckers.

Most truckers, including myself, supplemented their access to truck stop foodstuffs with purchases at Walmart or grocery stores, storing these goods in the small refrigerator that almost all sleepers have and preparing meals in the microwave that is also quite prevalent in semi sleeper units. My own diet generally consisted of one real meal each day, then grazing on snacks, mostly nuts and fruit, the rest of the day. Interestingly, I saw very little consumption of alcohol on the road. Beer and wine were available at the truck stops, but I witnessed very limited purchase or consumption of them by my fellow drivers. Though I regularly drink wine with dinner and occasionally imbibe a beer or hard liquor drink while at home, I consumed no alcohol while on the road. In part, that was because Swift has very stringent policies about such consumption—none within twelve hours of driving. I also avoided alcohol because I was intentionally dieting during my stint with Swift, and alcohol just didn't fit the diet. Incidentally, my dieting was more successful than I had anticipated; despite very limited exercise opportunities, I lost twenty pounds in my five months of driving for Swift.

Many of the TA and Petro truck stops, two sister businesses run by the TravelCenters of America company, have maintained cafeteria-style restaurants in many of their truck stops. TAs have Country Pride restaurants, and Petros have Iron Skillet restaurants, and they have very similar menus and services. I would often plan to hit one of these stops for my one major meal of the day. I personally think their breakfast is the best part of their menu, and I would try to schedule my day's driving to get an early start, drive for a few hours, and have a late, ample breakfast at a Country Pride. Every day, they serve a fixed menu but also provide a serve-yourself all-you-can-eat buffet, which includes a very nice and quite complete salad bar. On Sundays, they amplify the buffet and seem to attract a good number of locals for their Sunday dinner. They also have an all-you-can-eat fish fry on Friday—a tradition, I'm sure, from the long-past prohibition on meat for Catholics on Friday. Eating at one of these restaurants is truly a blast from the past. The menu is standard mid-American midcentury fare, and, yes, it does include chicken fried steak. Of course, I ordered it a couple of times, but it did not appear to be a big seller, either to me or to others. More frequently, my fellow drivers and I favored a substantial salad, perhaps a bowl of soup (generally from a selection of three that varied from day to day) and the buffet, all of which cost in the ten-dollar range.

On a number of occasions, I chose to go off campus for dinner. In Atlanta, Seattle, Sioux Falls, Bakersfield, Salt Lake City, and Laramie, I either walked or caught a cab or Uber to a nearby restaurant to have an upscale meal. On one California trip, I parked in a Swift terminal in Ontario, California, just outside of Los Angeles, rented a car, and visited friends in San Diego for a couple of days before getting back on the road. For the last three weeks of my tenure with Swift, my wife, Mary Jane, joined me over the road. Similar to my San Diego escapade, she and I took a brief detour to dine with friends in Saint Paul, Minnesota, on a trip taking a load to Wisconsin. I'm sort of a foodie, so this was an opportunity for me to taste, as well as see, a bit of the country. Oh, and by the way, it was on the road that I discovered my new favorite chain restaurant, the Black Bear restaurants. They're pretty much limited to the Pacific Northwest, but I recommend them if you happen to come across one. They're great for breakfast, lunch, or dinner, to which I can attest because I tried all three meals. And their fresh-squeezed orange juice is to die for.

All of which is to say that, despite the limited food options, I found it quite possible to eat enjoyably, healthy, and wise while driving over the road.

CHAPTER 9
AMERICA'S INFRASTRUCTURE—
ROADS AND BRIDGES

DURING THE 2016 presidential election cycle, both candidates made a big deal out of the need to address America's deteriorating infrastructure. While many feared that this may have simply been campaign rhetoric, once elected President Trump maintained that investing in improvements in the country's infrastructure, be it highways, bridges, airports, dams, or pipelines, would remain a high priority for him, though significant investments in this agenda never actually materialized. And, in fact, our infrastructure needs were hardly a new discovery. In the American Recovery and Reinvestment Act of 2009, which you will remember was a significant portion of the successful effort of the federal government to pull us out of the Great Recession, billions of federal dollars were invested in shovel-ready projects addressing serious infrastructure needs across the nation.

Despite those efforts, however, we still face huge infrastructure issues. From a truck driver's perspective, these are quite obvious as you travel our nation's highways and byways. Some argue that this is just the nature of things; we built great highways in the mid-twentieth century, and now they need attention. While there is some truth to this, I have had the good fortune of traveling throughout the world, and I can tell you that this is not a universal problem. China is building a highway system that puts ours to shame. Italy, which has far more public finance problems than does America, has a great highway system. Australia, a country that, like America, has great expanses and thus provides a strong national highway system, does a much better job of doing so than does America. While I personally have not been a great fan of President Trump's "make America great again" theme, because I truly believe America remains a great country, it is an appropriate theme for our infrastructure, which simply is no longer great.

First, I want to address our once-great interstate highway system. Much of it just stinks. Some sections are so bad that they actually represent safety hazards. There is a section of I-40, west of Flagstaff, Arizona, that is so torn up it is hard to hold a semi on the road. There was a section of I-15 north of Salt Lake City that was so pocked with potholes that I and many other drivers actually drove on the shoulder of the highway to avoid damage or worse. A section of I-95 West traveling beside Lake Kachess on Snoqualmie Pass in Washington state is almost impossible for a truck to safely traverse, particularly in winter weather when snow abounds; because the highway is under construction, three lanes have been compressed into two, both of which are in terrible condition, with lanes that have confusing lines and are simply too narrow for trucks to safely travel, especially at highway speeds. And then there is South Carolina, where the interstates are just rotten from one end to the other.

One of the rules of the road for truckers is that they are supposed to stay in the slow lane, except to pass. Actually, that is a rule in many states for all vehicles, be they trucks or four-wheelers, but it is a general rule for truckers across the country. And, in fact, our interstates and most multilane byways are designed with this in mind, paving the slow (outside) lane deeper than the fast (inside) lane in order to handle the extra weight of trucks. But these initial construction efforts only go so far. The combination of weather and heavy truck traffic ultimately takes its toll, and the roads deteriorate.

What I find interesting, however, is that the highways in some states are in terrible condition, while they are generally quite good in other states. Iowa and Nebraska, for example, generally have quite good highways. Part of the reason for this is the way in which the interstate highway system is financed. While the federal government financed the initial construction of the system and continues to finance a major portion of the reconstruction of the system, maintaining the system is the responsibility of the states. Drawing a line between what is construction and thus a federal responsibility and what is maintenance and thus a state responsibility is sometimes a bit sketchy. Today, the federal government is providing about 37.5 percent of the funding going into the interstate system, and states are funding the remaining 62.5 percent of funding. Though some states argue that they bear an unusual burden because of unique circumstances, like mountainous territory and more frequent inclement weather, I suspect that the states with lousy portions of the highway system simply haven't provided the funding necessary to maintain their sections of the interstate highways. Clearly, however, the federal government has not held up its share of the bargain either, and in this case, the reason is very clear; the feds have been unwilling to up the gas tax that provides the funds for reconstruction. The current 18.5 cents per gallon federal gas tax, which is the primary source for such federal funds, has not been increased since 1993. Had it simply been increased by the rate of inflation (as measured by the consumer price index) it would now be 36.75 cents per gallon, and there would be a lot more funding available to repair and replace our federally funded roads and bridges. I know, I know—taxes are bad, even though the goods and services they provide are generally good. In this case, though, our deflated cents make no sense.

And if our roads aren't bad enough, our bridges are in even worse shape. This is true in both our interstate system and our many other byways throughout the country. The Federal Highway Administration estimates that 71,000 (12 percent) of America's bridges are structurally deficient. As a trucker, knowing every heavy load I carry over one of these bridges is risky business, this eminent safety hazard suggests that the president's focus on infrastructure must remain a high priority.

In addition to the simple fact that many bridges are structurally deficient and need to be replaced, there is another annoying and damaging issue with bridges. Apparently, some construction engineers don't quite understand that bridges and roads should abut each other. Makes sense, right? Well, in many places, it simply isn't so. And again, it varies hugely from state to state. In Nebraska and Iowa, for example, the transition from road to bridge and back again is quite smooth. But in states like Washington, Oregon, and Colorado, there can be quite a gap in the height of the road and bridge. In a car, this gap is hardly noticeable because the springs and shock absorbers can adequately moderate the bump. In a semi, however, the weight of the tractor and trailer are so substantial that the suspension system can't fully absorb the shock, giving the truck and its driver quite a ride over almost every road. I've been tempted, and may still do so, to send a letter of kudos to the engineering schools at the Land Grant Universities in states that seem to understand that roads should transition smoothly onto bridges, and a somewhat different letter to such programs in states that simply don't seem to teach this in their construction engineering programs. Unfortunately, my alma mater, Washington State University, which I love dearly, would not be the beneficiary of my letter of kudos, because Washington's highways are among the worst in this transgression.

All of which is to affirm the last two presidents' concerns about our nation's degraded highways and bridges. If only Congress could get the message. And, by the way, I understand that correcting this will cost more than we have dedicated in the past and that this means increasing taxes to get the job done. But, damnit, our highways are an essential public good and thus both deserve and require public financing.

CHAPTER 10
R-E-S-P-E-C-T OR LACK THEREOF

"RESPECT," WRITTEN BY Otis Redding and perhaps the great Aretha Franklin's most famous recording, captured so much attention not only because of its amazing and captivating rhythm and musicality but also because of its compelling lyrics—lyrics that capture what we all want and need: "All I'm askin' is for a little respect ... just a little bit." And it's no different for truck drivers.

The definition of respect I like the best from *The American Heritage Dictionary* is "the willingness to show appreciation and consideration; a feeling of deferential regard, esteem." My parents were great at showing respect for others, no matter what their station in life—that is, as long as the respect was earned and deserved. I personally believe that my folks had it right; everyone who has earned it deserves respect.

That's not how it works for many truck drivers, however. Far too often, others treat truck drivers like dirt. And, indeed, some of my best friends fall into this category. I didn't notice this when I told people that I intended to become a truck driver, I suspect because many of them just thought I was blowing smoke. When I actually began driving, however, I found many of my friends thought that what I was doing was "beneath me" somehow. That I was "better than that." And while on the road, it became evident that this attitude toward truck drivers, though not universal to be sure, was quite prevalent.

Certainly, not all truck drivers deserve respect from others. Some truckers are hotheads, jerks as I detailed in previous chapters, or dangerous drivers, and they don't deserve your respect. They certainly don't have mine. But the huge majority of truck drivers are competent, decent, and conscientious. These men and women keep American commerce working, and do so for the most part safely and courteously, which by my definition means they deserve your respect. They certainly have mine.

So, who disrespects truck drivers? I've already mentioned the condescension of the professional class, of which I have been a member most of my life. I'll discuss in a later chapter how this lack of respect has created a climate among many truck drivers that drives them toward a philosophy of alienation from our nation's "best and brightest," or at least those of us who think we are.

But "we" are not the only people who regularly disrespect truckers, whether realizing it or not. Perhaps the greatest disrespect, which I have referred to previously, comes from the customers that truckers serve, specifically the shipping and receiving points around the nation. Some of the lack of respect comes directly from the staff within the warehouses where shipping and receiving occurs. This varies hugely in the industry. Many of the shipping and receiving offices have exceptionally competent and courteous staff, well trained to interact with the hordes of truckers they must deal with every day. Some shops, however, could give a damn. Ofttimes, their lack of courtesy is simply a function of disorganization, with lack of communication between the staff that interact directly with the truckers and those behind the scene in the warehouse who ultimately load or unload. Too often, however, it is simply lousy attitudes of the shipping and receiving staff; it's as if they don't want to be bothered. They don't know when the load might be loaded or unloaded, and they don't care; quit bugging them. They don't know why you don't know their unique procedures, which vary substantially from one warehouse to another, and have little patience for your lack of knowledge. They either don't know how to give clear instructions or simply prefer not to do so. And too often, they are just plain surly or dismissive.

Even more disrespectful are the myriad ways in which customer companies' business processes simply diss truck drivers. I've already mentioned how some companies routinely delay either receiving or loading trucks for hours on end. This conveniently serves the customer's needs, but it costs the trucker both time and money (and often preciously needed sleep). Local work rules can also unintentionally show disrespect. On many occasions, loading or unloading my trailer would be in process, perhaps just minutes away from completion, when time for break or lunch came, and the lumper crew disappeared for up to an hour. Couldn't such work rules be adjusted to allow for breaks and meals between loads?

In addition, some DOT rules and regulations demonstrate a lack of respect for truck drivers. I understand and actually appreciate the time limits placed on drivers—no more than eight hours behind the wheel without a break, no more than eleven hours driving without a ten-hour break to rest, and no more than fourteen hours on duty without the ten-hour break. Sometimes, however, these just don't make sense. If, for example, you get stuck in a warehouse lot for a number of hours, without permission to leave your truck, thus requiring that your entire time to be recorded as on duty, you are simply going to run out of duty time. This leads to either a violation of the DOT regulation or some "clever" manipulations to make sure you don't. Wouldn't it make sense for DOT to respect drivers enough to allow them to make exceptions to the rules, with appropriate documentation, so that drivers' logs were a more accurate reflection of the real world? Drivers who regularly break the rules by "cleverly" driving too many hours deserve no respect and should be held responsible. But drivers who simply get caught in an impossible catch-22 should be respected enough to professionally manage their way out of the circumstance, albeit with documentation of their efforts. For forty years prior to my truck-driving days, I managed other people. And I know that I got much greater productivity from those I managed when I respected them for their professional behavior and gave them the leeway to demonstrate it. The same would be true for truck drivers, were they respected enough to accept such responsibility.

While truck drivers experience the lack of respect I have described above, and it certainly helps one understand their general philosophy of life, they do often actually receive respect in other realms. First and foremost, they generally receive respect from one another. While there are a few drivers who love to bitch and moan about other drivers, most drivers treat one another quite nicely. When I could benefit from the assistance of another driver, be it in guiding me into a tight parking spot or loading dock or in advising me about driving conditions ahead, I could always find it, generally with a friendly face attached. And on the road, truckers will almost always provide room for another trucker to merge into traffic or between lanes and will often acknowledge your presence with a wave or a smile.

Truckers also receive great respect at the truck stops. Sure, this is because respect garners more business, but nonetheless, it is there in spades. The truck stop facilities, in general, are designed to respect truck drivers in a variety of ways: with convenient parking, ample fueling bays, convenience stores stocked to truly serve the truck drivers, excellent shower facilities, professional driver lounges, and a staff that caters conscientiously to the drivers. Staff at the truck stops refer to you as "professional truck drivers" and treat you as such. Some of the larger facilities go even further, with massage therapists, barbers, dentists, and chiropractors. I can't remember being in a truck stop where the staff wasn't as pleasant as could be, and that had to be an acquired skill for many of the women staff who were incessantly being hit on by the natural chauvinism of many male truck drivers.

CHAPTER 11
THE TRUCK-DRIVING CULTURE

WHEN TALKING TO folks about truck driving and the community of truckers, I am often asked about the truck-driving culture. Truth be told, there isn't a particularly unique truck-driving culture because the community of truckers is so diverse. It may have been that years ago, truck drivers were a more homogeneous lot, but today, truck drivers are so numerous and come from such diverse backgrounds that it is hard to accurately capture it as a community with its own culture.

The nature of truck driving, however, does attract and create a cadre of folks with some characteristics more dominant than are reflected in American culture as a whole. Driving over the road is a solitary life unless you are one of the fortunate couples (married or not) that share life as team drivers. To make a good living as a truck driver (and contrary to articles in the *Economist* and the *New York Times*, truck drivers can make a good living), you must be dedicated to spending almost all of your time on the road. DOT has established that truckers can't drive for a maximum of more than seventy hours in any eight-day period, though most truckers don't see this as a maximum but as an expectation if they want to make a good living. And the culmination of your seventy hours often doesn't comfortably find you home, so very often, your thirty-four-hour required layover, known as a reset, is on the road, not at home.

This work schedule doesn't lend itself to a robust family life. In the five months I drove for Swift, I missed Christmas, New Year's, my birthday, and Easter and in total had six days off at home. I'm not complaining, just explaining. This simply isn't a lifestyle conducive to being a good husband and father.

From my observations, truckers fall into four categories with regard to this lifestyle. Many, if not most, are very comfortable because they are basically loners. I don't say that pejoratively, just honestly. These people enjoy the solitude of being alone on the road. To some extent, I fit comfortably into this category while working for Swift. My best friend during that time was my Freightliner Cascadia; I enjoyed her and treated her well, as she did to me. It was a wonderful time of my life. Yes, I missed my family, particularly my wife, but my wife and I were solid in our relationship, and this wasn't for us a long-term lifetime decision.

For most truckers who look at this as a long-term work life decision, they accept but don't relish the loneliness of driving. They find ways to manage their life both within their work and outside of it as best they can, recognizing the tradeoffs necessary and finding reasonable accommodations along the way. My mentor, Ed, fit into this category. He talked freely about not enjoying the lonely life, but he chose it because it provided a fairly lucrative income. He accommodated by talking with his estranged wife, daughter, son, brother, and lady friends regularly on the phone. Yes, he was one of those who regularly walked around with the headphones on his noggin. He also admitted that, in part, he mentored new truck drivers like me so that he would have company in the cab. He also benefited from being a rather gregarious guy who could easily pick up conversation with other drivers at the truck stops.

Now, having said that this cadre of drivers often find ways to make this lifestyle work, many never quite find the balance. I regularly heard drivers talking about the difficulties of maintaining a strong marriage (many referred to their numerous marriages). Others spoke about troubles in establishing decent relationships with their children, particularly with teenage children.

A lot of drivers fall into a third category, which is they simply choose a tract other than over-the-road driving. Many simply quit over-the-road driving and opt for local delivery work. Local work generally isn't as lucrative as over the road and can be a bit boring, but it is often more steady work and provides more opportunities for regular family life. A variant on this is referred to as driving a "dedicated route," where an over-the-road driver has a specific route with a very predictable schedule. I had a friend who drove for Swift who had a dedicated Target run from Pueblo, Colorado, to Salt Lake City and return. He would travel out one day, return the next, and then have a day off. These dedicated routes are cherished assignments and generally go to the most experienced drivers who have earned the opportunity.

And, finally, there are those drivers who just don't like the job because of the basic nature of the task. I couldn't believe the number of drivers I would listen to at the truck stops who just plain hated their job because of the nature of the beast. Many of these folks appear to have gotten into truck driving because it was one of the few ways they could make a decent living, perhaps because they lacked the education and credentials to qualify for other types of work, but never really took to the job. For others, they had entered the field of work with romantic visions of what truck driving would be like, only to find that it was not what they had envisioned and was quite hard work.

Having earlier stated that there is no truck-driving culture, it is true that very few truck drivers would fit, either in reality or in their own minds, into the upper-middle class of American life. Most have decent but still modest incomes, sufficient to keep their heads above water but not enough to get ahead or to plan much for the future. Most have limited education; though some are college educated, most are not. And virtually all truck drivers work hard. While most truck drivers would describe themselves as middle-class Americans, they are probably more accurately described as working-class Americans. And their attitudes and attributes fit this general characterization. Because they work hard in a profession where jobs are relatively plentiful, many have quite a bit of contempt for the welfare system. They believe that welfare supports lazy people who choose not to work. They also have a fair bit of contempt for the professional class, of which I had previously been a part, because they feel that these people don't work any harder than they do but earn a lot more just because they went to college and are connected. Not surprisingly, therefore, they are not very keen on education, per se, which they believe simply creates a leisure class that lives the easy life on the backs of those who do real work. So, they don't think much of either those Americans who are lower on the totem pole of society than they are or those who have climbed the pole higher. And they are particularly resentful of those who were born into wealth and have the gall to castigate those who were not.

Not surprisingly, most of the truck drivers I met had quite different perspectives on the world, including the world of politics, than do I or than do most of the folks with whom I have lived, loved, and played throughout my life. I'll talk more about these differences later.

There was also another bifurcation within the community of truck drivers, which I describe as the kempt and unkempt. Based on the discussions about trucking I have had with those individuals basically unfamiliar with trucking and truckers attire, it appears that most folks believe that all truckers are slobs. And, indeed, many truck drivers, perhaps even most (I never did a tally) dress mighty casually. Many favor cargo shorts over jeans or slacks because they are comfortable. And a number sport tank tops so they can display their tattoos. Quite often, those who prefer such attire do so to accommodate rather rotund bodies, reflecting the general American fetish with obesity. The cab of their tractor often reflects similar traits.

On the other hand, many truck drivers are strack in their appearance and apparel. Not surprisingly, many of these folks are ex-military, but this is also true of many company drivers who are required to maintain certain levels of decorum in dress, some of which actually provide uniforms. For many, however, it is simply an issue of pride in their profession. My mentor, Ed, kept a very clean cab and dressed quite nicely, but he did so just because he liked to look good and felt it was the most appropriate thing to do. I felt much the same as Ed, which helped make our short partnership work well.

One common misperception about truck drivers is that they tend to be dirty and odoriferous. Sure, drivers sometimes get dirty, particularly in the winter, because working outside the tractor—connecting the trailer, inspecting the vehicle, fueling, and so on—can be less than tidy processes, but in general, the majority of truck drivers stay as clean as possible, and the truck stops foster this by providing very nice and affordable shower rooms. Now, that hasn't always been the case. In conversation with one old-timer one evening in Snoqualmie, Washington, he said that in the old days, back in the twentieth century, the Snoqualmie truck stop's shower was an outdoor contraption with a showerhead hanging over a pallet that served as the drain, and in the winter, you had to beware of ice—though I admit that this sounded a bit like the tales we all heard (or told) about having to walk to school barefooted and uphill both directions.

In general, I would say that truck drivers dressed much like the crowds you might see in almost any American airport—some nicely dressed, many not so much—and generally for the same reasons, those being comfort, taste, or lack thereof.

Another misperception about truck drivers and truck stops is that they are keen on prostitution. That was certainly not my experience. In my time driving for Swift, I believe that only once did I see a true lizard (the trucker term for a prostitute). That was in

Denver at a TA truck stop where I witnessed the truck stop's security officer escorting an obviously inebriated lizard off the grounds. Now, that's not universally the case, and my fellow truck drivers told me that it certainly isn't in New Jersey and Oregon, where prostitution is supposedly rampant. I have also heard that truck drivers are the most prevalent patrons of adult bookstores, and the frequent location of these establishments close to truck stops would tend to support that presumption. And virtually every longtime truck driver can tell stories. But I simply didn't see it. And, in fact, Swift's orientation warned drivers about the dangers of lizards and was particularly strong in its concerns about human trafficking and what we should do if we ever thought we were witnessing it.

So, the community of truck drivers is not that different from America at large. It is diverse, working class, and interested more in today than tomorrow. It has people of exceptionally high character and many who aren't, just like the rest of America. And it has all of the positive and negative attributes of a culture so mixed.

CHAPTER 12
DIFFERENT PERSPECTIVES— HOW GOOD PEOPLE CAN SUPPORT DONALD TRUMP

I FULLY EXPECTED that the truck-driving community I was entering would carry different perspectives than I have about American life and politics, and the reality certainly met my expectations. Truckers, be they drivers, staff supporting the trade, or trucking company executives, almost universally had substantially different perspectives than I did. And part of my intrigue about becoming a truck driver was to explore the reasons and rationale behind these differing perspectives. This exploration turned out to be one of the most informative and enlightening aspects of my truck-driving career. I pursued this interest primarily by listening and conversing, not by arguing. Even to the extent that many with whom I conversed probably didn't even perceive my own perspective. I wanted to learn from them, not convert them. While my colleagues never convinced me that my ideology was wrong, I did come to understand how good people can support Donald Trump.

First, I should confess to you a bit about my own perspectives and how my life has helped shape them. I grew up in a family of very modest means in a rural community in north central Washington State. My dad was a carpenter, and my mom ran a small motel that we owned. I worked from the age of twelve, was a good student, and went to college, as did both of my sisters. Although my parents had both dropped out of school because of the Depression—Mom from college, Dad from high school—they highly valued college and were going to make sure we became well educated, not only because an education could provide us with better financial circumstances than they had but because the life of the mind can provide so many other advantages to living the good life. And we have all benefited immeasurably from their insight. I certainly live the good life. After college, I was drafted and spent fourteen months in Vietnam. Upon leaving the army, I continued to pursue my education, ultimately receiving a doctorate in education from Stanford University, which opened up opportunities that I could hardly have ever imagined. Financially, my family is secure. I benefit from good health, a wonderful marriage of more than fifty years, and a breadth of experiences and opportunities that make life a joy. My life is the American dream, so as you might expect, I'm rather keen on America.

My career prior to truck driving was spent working within or around state and federal government, specifically focusing on college and university policy and practice. I ran state government agencies in Minnesota and Colorado and worked for both the Congress and the Clinton administration at the federal level. Not surprisingly, therefore, I think I know a good bit about government and basically believe in it. The late great political scientist James Q. Wilson once quipped that "once politics was about only a few things; today, it is about nearly everything," and this closely fits my worldview as well.

Obviously, both by life experience and job experience, my perspective has been shaped by fundamentally different forces than is the case for most truck drivers. Just because it is different, however, makes it neither necessarily superior nor correct. Most of the truck drivers I met are very nice people. Yes, many of them see the world differently than I do, and I truly believe some of them even have abhorrent attitudes about certain modern issues, like race, sexuality, gender relationships, and so on, but in almost all cases, these result from perspectives developed under very different circumstances than those I experienced, and, right or wrong, their perspectives can be understood in that context.

So, how is it that these basically good people can support Donald Trump, who I believe, as do most of my closest friends, is shamefully and disgustingly an abhorrent, ideologically vacant, simpleminded, narcissistic, crude, misogynistic liar, yet he became president of the United States, elected at least in part by these "good people." Why?

Well, in part it was because they are patriotic Americans, and they felt it was about time we elected someone who would speak up for America. I must tell you, I personally find President Trump's "make America great again" slogan offensive. As I mentioned earlier, I have lived the American dream. Frankly, I deserved it because I worked mighty hard to achieve it. I was able to get it, so I truly believe that America is great; indeed, it is about as great as it ever has been. We can certainly do better, particularly for lower- and middle-class Americans and with many within our various communities of color, but I travel a good bit, and I can tell you that America remains the greatest nation in the world and has the greatest potential for becoming even greater. Certainly, Donald Trump couldn't and didn't lead us there with his asinine ideas about the environment, people of color, trickle-down economics, militarism (even though he ducked military service himself), and world isolationism, but with better leadership, we can become an even better country.

My truck-driver colleagues saw the world much differently than this. What I saw as a rather stupid bully, they saw as a forthright advocate for the America they dream of, one in which they would be paid what they are worth, where others aren't taking their jobs, and where politicians aren't always dissing America, whether these dreams are myth or reality. What I saw as bullying, they saw as Trump standing up to the plutocrats. And whom they saw as plutocrats, I see as intelligent, learned, often wise people worth listening to and following.

When I would question their support for an inveterate liar, their response generally was that, hey, all politicians are liars, so what's the big deal. When presented with evidence that his lying was more pervasive and more outrageous, they would say that was just my buying the corrupt media's fake news. And, unfortunately, there is enough veracity in what they say to convince them that they are correct. Without doubt, Hillary Clinton's campaign, which I actually voluntarily worked for, while not dishonest in the same vein of candidate Trump, was far less transparent about some issues than even I was comfortable with. And the need for news channels to simply fill time has led to far too much talk about possible transgressions than real evidence of such transgressions on the part of Trump, both as a candidate and as the president. Of course, this abundance of fact-free discussion goes both ways, with Fox news actually fabricating stories, though they are only a bit more shameful than some other news networks.

Perhaps the area I had the most difficulty reconciling were the perspectives that differed with mine on issues of bigotry. Some of my trucker colleagues simply refused to accept that President Trump's comments were racist or sexist. Others would simply agree with the bigoted perspective. There is a great deal of anti-immigrant agreement with Trump among many truck drivers. Much of this is frankly ill informed, but it is mighty prevalent. They believe Mexicans are taking jobs from Americans and helping to depress wages for moderate-income jobs. Many believe that most black people are lazy, don't want to work, and are living high off the hog on welfare. Many would like to see a homogeneous (meaning white) America again. Now, I know for a fact that these perspectives are factually baseless and barbaric, but they account for why the president is so popular among many of my fellow drivers. I found this particularly interesting, given the tremendous racial, ethnic, and cultural diversity within the truck-driving community.

Trump's misogynistic tendencies also tend not to bother many truck drivers. In part, this is because many of them basically share these tendencies. Many have also been married numerous times, have ongoing affairs, found his comments about grabbing pussy to be humorous rather than crude and offensive, and enjoy ogling women themselves.

What I see as narcissism, they saw as the confidence of a successful self-made businessman willing to be a renegade revolutionary against the ruling class. When I pointed out to them that he was hardly a self-made success, having grown up with a silver spoon in his mouth and having been fronted millions by his father to go into the real estate business, they simply said that's not their understanding. And when I brought up the evidence of his charlatan business practices, stiffing contractors, declaring bankruptcy multiple times, and hiring illegal immigrants, they simply said that's the way business is conducted in New York.

And they "knew" this from viewing Fox news and following suggested blogs and news outlets online that do, in fact, provide fake news.

All of which suggests that they simply follow the instincts of their experiences in the formulation of their perspectives, just as my friends and I are following our quite different instincts and perspectives. I continue to believe that mine are more informed and reasonable, but they would expect nothing less of one of the professional class.

And I remain perplexed about how to bring good people with such different perspectives together to find some common ground.

CHAPTER 13
RIDING SHOTGUN WITH MY LATE-TO-THE-GAME TRUCKER HUSBAND—A SLIGHTLY DIFFERENT PERSPECTIVE

AS FAR BACK as I can remember in our marriage, and that's many years now, Dave has always been fascinated with big rig trucks. Once when we were gearing up for a move and had enlisted the help of a friend, the two of them talked about renting a huge moving van. For two reasons, this seemed ridiculous. First, we didn't have all that many possessions, and secondly, we were moving a few doors up the block. Nonetheless, it tickled their imaginations to dream this grand plan. Suffice it to say that their true desire, after spending a couple of quick hours actually moving our household, was to simply drive a really big truck around, acting like they knew what they were doing, and then brag to their friends about this superb experience. In the end, they rented a sizeable dolly that handled the task quite nicely.

Ever after that, Dave made frequent references to driving an eighteen-wheeler, and over the years, I began to realize that this desire was gaining momentum. At one point, I gave him a birthday gift of a mini-lesson at US Truck Driving School near Denver. The whole family went along; we all had a great time even though the lesson never ventured outside the truck yard. Then, as Dave was looking at an actual retirement date from his entire career spent in higher education, his talk of trucking picked up considerably. This did not go unnoticed by his friends, colleagues, and wife, all of whom began asking specifics of his new line of work, which in turn apparently created some pressure to follow through. And he has done that in a big way.

Thus followed CDL training at Aims Community College in Greeley, Colorado, obtaining the CDL (very big day for him—almost on par with getting his college graduate degrees), a job search, and an internship with Swift Transportation, followed by assignment of his own truck and several months on the road as a real-deal Swift trucker. That is how I came to accompany him for several weeks in a cross-country and back ride-along.

Create Your Own Adventure

In mid-March, Dave had been driving his truck for a steady three months with very few days off. He had always said he'd like to take me along, so voila! With his payment of a small amount of money to cover additional insurance, I was ready to go. The whole idea had huge appeal for me. I like road trips, seeing new places, a dose of adventure, and the idea of living in a contained space without the need for a lot of belongings or other clutter that can easily consume one in the home setting. Furthermore, I like being with Dave and was anxious to support him in this long-held fantasy. Pulling together an appropriate wardrobe and other necessities took only a few minutes, and before I knew it, there we were, sitting together in the cab at Swift's Denver terminal.

During CDL training, he had come home frequently listing off newly acquired terminology and tractor/trailer parts, but during the real checkout at the terminal, I caught the gleeful pride in his voice as he ran through these same items. At some points, he stopped and demonstrated how parts could move or interlock, or possibly fail (yikes), while looking sternly at me as though I might need this knowledge somewhere down the road. Good luck there!

We headed north to Wyoming, a state that I have traversed many times, always while thinking just how much of the traffic consists of trucks—pickups, light and heavy, larger service vans, trucks used in construction, equipment and livestock carriers, tankers, on and on, but especially, and overwhelmingly, eighteen-wheelers. And now we were part of this massive caravan! There are numerous points in Wyoming where one can scan an undulating ribbon of highway far toward the horizon, and it seems that 80 percent of what can be seen moving along is trucks. So, logically, this state, despite its low population, has lots of highway pull-outs, weigh stations, and rest and truck stops. This last facility was part of the lore I was very curious about.

The TA truck stop where I spent my initial night was altogether typical. It consisted of numerous gas pumps, separated for trucks and autos, a lengthy truck scale, a medium-sized restaurant attached to a convenience store, a few mechanical work bays advertised as being open twenty-four hours a day, and a huge parking lot where possibly one hundred trucks were pulled side by side, ready to spend the night. The sound of reefer motors droned away as we bedded down and I tried to put out of mind that the bathroom, should I need it, was a chilly two-block walk away.

Trucker Hours

A long-haul trucker's *on* shift may begin any time of the day or night and lasts varying hours depending where he or she may be on the accumulative clock. (See Dave's notes.) During my time on the road, we usually began sometime in the morning, though that varied from before dawn until close to noon. There were nights when we drove almost straight through, but also a couple of days when we didn't travel at all. A long hauler needs to become flexible about work hours and efficient in using downtime as well.

Sleeping/living in the cab is much like camping but with better headroom than a tent. Minimal square footage utilizes every nook and cranny for purposeful duty. Ours, the bare-bones model, consisted of two extra-long bunks, a closet for hanging clothes, a compact refrigerator, a food and dish cupboard, a desk doubling as a small table, and a couple of other small storage compartments. Heavy-duty curtains can be drawn between the drive and sleeping portions of the cab, as well as across all cab windows, allowing for privacy and light diversion.

Morning after my first on-the-road sleepover came very quickly. (This riding shotgun is exhausting!) We had a fair amount of mileage to cover before our 8:00 a.m. scheduled delivery, so we had to hit the interstate well before dawn. In true slacker style though, I barely roused myself before deciding I couldn't face the dark of day so snuggled down for more sleep. Eighty miles down the road, I woke up for real to catch a beautiful sunrise, made more so by the scarcity of visible life anywhere within view. Sometimes it really does feel like you have left humanity behind. Dave tells me that it's these quiet hours on the road that he relishes, helping convince him that his dream job is living up to his expectations.

Making Deliveries

Encountering my first delivery, near Ogden, Utah, I was astounded at the size of the Associated Foods Distribution Center. One doesn't have to drive very far away from any larger American city, or even in rural areas along major highways, to see these, but up close, you really feel the enormity of the operation. Of the large variety, there might be more than two hundred loading docks, and in the surrounding parking lots, you see as many or more trailers waiting to be picked up. Inside this one, the chilly temperature hits us as we enter, even though it's not at all warm outside. Passing a double row of forklifts at the ready, the brightly lit interior exposes industrial shelving that reaches what seems a couple of stories high and stretches two football fields long. What a monstrous place! Still, it seems that relatively few people work within its massive confines. Later on, we would deliver and pick up loads at widely varying sized warehouses and processing plants. For some reason, I curiously wanted to figure out how many employees might work within each location, but I never came up with any kind of calculating formula. For sure there's activity around the clock, but maybe not employing large numbers of people.

The workers who drive the forklifts that load and unload trucks have the undignified name of *lumpers*. Despite the image of slugs, made more so by the heavy, insulated clothing they wear, when it comes time for them to begin driving, they can scramble those lifts around quickly. Looking them up on an occupational wage scale, I see that their average hourly pay is $13.32.

This delivery turned out to be a "dry drop," one where the trailer was simply placed in the outer lot for later unloading, followed by our picking up another one, empty it turned out, for the next segment of our journey. Most of Dave's cargo was food of different sorts—whole loads of meat, pastries, candy, yogurt, frozen veggies, potpies, soup— which necessitated the refrigerated unit, which in turn meant keeping watch on a second gauge so that both truck and reefer tanks were filled and ready for the drive ahead.

Picking up a Load

To my observation, these procedures appear way more complicated than the deliveries. While both involve the tricky maneuvers of backing or pulling the trailer into what seems like impossibly narrow spaces, following the loading procedure, the driver has to make certain it is balanced. (See Dave's notes.) With luck, the loading team does their part to achieve this, but still the driver must adjust the axles (who knew this was even possible?) and then go to a truck weigh station, usually at the truck stop, because doing so at the loading facility would be a conflict of interest (again, who knew?) to ascertain if the load is indeed legal. For novice drivers, this might require several attempts, with a lot of short hops forward, then abrupt halts, immediately followed by much banging and clatter as iron parts slip into place. When a driver thinks they've hit the proper adjustment, they usually hop down and trot back to the rear carriage to eyeball the wheel placement. Once, Dave had to go through these steps eight different times to balance his load. Two weeks later, when he revisited the same scales for this purpose, the weight-check ladies remembered him instantly. Apparently he'd set some sort of dubious high mark. This time though, we breezed through with a mere two weigh-ins.

Sometimes during my ride-along with Dave, when he needed someone to keep an eye on his axle adjustment or backing procedures, he'd ask me to go out to motion him into position. This too seemed dubious, in that I had no prior instruction and in fact have a lifelong confusion between right and left—lack of bilateral integration, someone termed it. And when little you gets behind that fifty-foot trailer, hidden as may be the case by the angle between cab and trailer, well, there's just a lot of different ways this whole scenario can end badly. But, oh well, I know how to wave my arms around, and as luck would have it, we occasionally backed into a dock without parked trucks on either side. A small bonus for a newbie trucker and his even greener assistant.

Trucker Support

In the cab between pickups and deliveries, I was beginning to feel right at home. Our routine, assuming we'd slept more or less normal nighttime hours, was to get up, dress, go into the rest or truck stop, complete our bathroom duties, get coffee, and return to the cab to review the day's travel. Sometimes we'd eat breakfast in the restaurant, but that meal was an easy one to handle in the truck—cereal with yogurt and fruit. Dave usually checked in with his team leader, though due to all the electronic monitoring devices on the Swift trucks, that person or someone else at the dispatch center always knew where we were. More than that, they also knew what type of facility we used to spend downtime, gas mileage, average speed, trailer weight, and if we were on schedule for our destination. Forget about that *Cannonball* duo who would veer off the highway whenever they could sniff out a bit of adventure or drama. We were being fully tracked.

It's difficult to imagine what long-haul trucking must have been like before GPS, the internet, and cell phones. I know that an era of CB radios existed, still does, but that's driver-to-driver contact, not supervision between headquarters and their truckers. So these days, as one travels along, there are intermittent notices reminding drivers of their progress, data that helps keep them safe, in compliance with road rules, and notified about events ahead. Some of this info is also used to calculate truckers' pay. Signals may go off in the cab; for example, if our truck ventured too far onto the right shoulder, a loud buzzer would sound. Dave told me that if a driver violated certain rules repeatedly, company citations would be issued. But on the extremely helpful side of this technology are the verbal instructions and admonitions the GPS provides, guiding one through unknown areas and to each exact delivery address. (Well ... most of the time. Read under "Communication.")

As the Miles Go By

I knew a NASA astronaut who made a couple of trips into space. When asked what he and his launch mates did when not handling flight operations, personal chores, or sleeping, he said they all loved looking out their windows and never tired of what they saw below. Well, an eighteen-wheeler certainly isn't a spacecraft, and while I had no official duties, I still felt the same way about my view from this high perch of the passenger seat. Some of the landscape was repetitious, but over the days, it changed dramatically. Prairies, agricultural properties, rolling hills, forests, rugged mountains, small towns, crowded urban areas, wide stretches of only pavement, housing of every sort—everything you know, and more, that's a part of American geography and culture.

We would keep an eye out for clues of weather ahead and speculate as to what drove the economy in places where it wasn't readily apparent. We learned of local attractions, political preferences, festivals, historical events, and the identity that people chose to give their towns: "Pride of the Prairie," "Best Little Town by a Dam Site," those both in Minnesota. Scattered along our route, we came across some downright oddities. At least that was what I thought when in southern Idaho we passed by what appeared to be a replica of Tara, the *Gone with the Wind* plantation home, facing the highway. It had a narrow driveway up to one side and a little landscaping, but the really distinguishing factor was its proximity to a small ramshackle farmhouse right next door and, surrounding both these houses, nothing but acres of dry grassland. What to make of this? Old house? New house?

Moving Along

After driving through solidly rural sections of Idaho, Oregon, and southeastern Washington, we headed for a Swift terminal outside Tacoma, our first location along the drive where we had a longer scheduled layover. For me, this meant the first shower in several days—heaven!—and the chance to spend an afternoon with a friend, who was as anxious to see our on-the-road home as I was to give her the official tour. With the extra downtime, we took public transit into Seattle and had a lovely casual dinner with our daughter and her husband. One of the things I was learning was that while truckers may go through major cities, their stops and layovers generally take place on the outer urban periphery. This makes complete sense when you stop to think that maneuvering and parking a big rig just doesn't lend itself to narrow city streets.

The next day, we slept in, anticipating a long stretch of working hours beginning with a midnight delivery just south of the terminal. We drove the short distance to encounter a great deal of activity in an extremely tight loading area. Dave was having difficulty backing his trailer into one of these skinny portals, and after several attempts, a watchful fellow trucker came up to his window and sort of motioned his willingness to help. Dave hopped down from the driver's seat, and this man climbed up, looking around the cab in some confusion; then he turned to me and in broken English shouted, "Auto!" several times, seemingly to ask for guidance. With no response from me, he threw his hands up in exasperation, then jammed the gears around, landing in reverse. For all his rough handling, it took only a couple of deft turns of the steering wheel, and the truck eased right into its loading dock.

Our delivery was followed by several hours of mostly urban driving. Traveling north on I-5, I was amazed at the volume of traffic flowing along at 3:30 a.m. Dave gave me the task of watching for a particular exit, which somehow we passed by with neither me nor the GPS giving notice. Maybe those dispatch people do sleep. By the time I realized this oversight, we were barreling along within a few miles of the Canadian border, no passports in hand, severely off track, Dave grumpy with fatigue, and no rest areas or truck stops in sight. Oh, and the gas needle pointed directly to empty. Finally we found a place to pull off the road, where we slept for less time than either of us wanted. Later that morning, we reoriented, picked up a load of frozen cranberries, got some breakfast, and turned eastward.

The following night, we pulled into a truck stop early enough to have a nice choice of parking spots, meaning easy to pull into. Truck stops vary in size, though many have lots that can hold seventy, eighty, or a hundred large trucks. Because the majority of truckers prefer to travel during the day and get off the road at night, these stops begin filling up later in the afternoon. Only a few of them have reserved spaces, to be had at a charge; otherwise, it's free parking on a first-come basis. Several times during our journey, when we arrived late at night, the only open spots were those that required extra-tricky maneuvering to occupy. It's always easier for a trucker to pull forward into a space rather than back into it.

At this North Bend, Washington, stop, we saw a female trucker whose image remains memorable indeed. Filling the gas tank of her fancy rig, she appeared to be fiftyish, with body ink everywhere, thinning, kinky hair, and a missing front tooth. She leaned on a cane, wore calf-length leggings and sneakers—the better to show off lower tattoos—and her flowing cape seemed the perfect complement to all the above. A cross between Ms. Frizzle and Strega Nona, I thought, for those familiar with children's literature.

The next day, we left the Pacific Northwest via Snoqualmie Pass, a highway through the Cascades that we both had traveled over many times before; but now, with snow and frost defining every single evergreen needle through the filtered sunlight, and the lack of traffic, never had it looked so beautiful.

Repairs

While descending a steep mountain pass in Idaho, the kind they mark with cautionary "use lower gear" signs and mention the angle of descent, we felt a soft thud and Dave wondered what it might be before, minutes later, signals in the cab indicated loss of hydraulic braking power. Thank goodness we were almost on flat terrain again. But this was serious business, so we pulled to a halt, and he phoned headquarters for help. One good thing about working for a large company like Swift is that they have quick access to something equivalent to Trucker AAA Roadside Assistance. And they pay for repairs. So, after a two-hour delay, we were safely back on the road again, moving east.

Dispatch outlined our route through Great Falls, Montana, which meant that we could see my brother, a truck aficionado from early childhood on. He's still got a small collection of toy trucks he used to push around while shifting their gears gutturally. Dave could hardly wait to show off his life-sized eighteen-wheeler. In short order though, while still many miles out from the Great Falls, the dispatcher changed routes on us, so, without that visit, onward we drove through southern Montana into South Dakota.

We now hit long stretches of uninhabited farm and prairie land, some of it designated Indian territory. There was plenty to keep our interest in the cab. Each morning, we tuned in to NPR while drinking coffee, accompanied by the tasty homemade biscotti a neighbor gave us as a road treat. We listened to murder mysteries, Neil Diamond and Willie Nelson CDs, and the NCAA basketball playoff games. Tuning up and down the radio dial, we heard a proliferation of religious programming, almost entirely of the evangelical variety. Also, because there was a dominance of truck traffic, I noticed the tendency for each to not only state their company name in bold lettering but also list some slogan that may define their business: WLA Inc., "Large Enough to Serve, Small Enough to Care"; CanXpress, "We're the Load Off Your Mind"; Karl's Transport, "God Delivers Us from Evil ... Karl's Delivers Everything Else." Dave's company, Swift, stated they were "The Best in Class." However, we were pulling a Central Refrigeration Trailer, and they had their own motto, "Dedicated Transportation Solutions." All this made one wonder who came up with those phrases, and did they spend a long time creating them or just shoot off whatever catchy thing came to mind? I noted the frequent use of the word "logistics" in the names and figured out it was the contemporary way of saying what was formerly "transport" or "transportation," just as we now use the word "metrics" to replace "numbers" or "data."

Truck Stop Food and Beyond

Back when Dave was just dreaming about being a truck driver, in order to put himself closer to the real culture, he would sometimes wrangle the whole family into our car and drive to Little America, Wyoming, for breakfast. This occurred at the same time our three girls weren't all that excited about spending extended periods with us, let alone two hours—each way!—during their coveted weekends. Therefore, we heard lots of grumbling, but Dave chalked these experiences up to quality family time, and now I think maybe the girls do too. The food was okay.

All these years later, okay sums up how I assess the truck stop food we ate on that trip. It's what you know to expect—basic meat platters, much of it fried, rounded out with a portion of vegetables and a good deal of starch. There were soup and salad bar offerings too, along with lots of desserts. Breakfasts might have been their best offering, if you can manage the heavy grease and, again, plentiful starch. This along with certain food items available in the adjacent convenience store could provide a balanced diet, though probably in the least healthful way possible. We generally ate only one full restaurant meal per day, supplemented by groceries we carried in the truck. During Dave's earlier months of driving, he lost fifteen pounds, following this same regime and eliminating all alcohol.

A couple of times along our route, we took transportation from a truck stop into the nearest town, searching for a dining change. Those meals, along with the different venue, were welcome relief, but for most long haulers, this would be prohibitively expensive and possibly too time-consuming.

On the plus side, truck stops offer products and services way beyond a parking space, their scales, fuel, and food. Their stores carry weather- and safety-related items (sunglasses, gloves, condoms, windshield cleaner, neon vests), basic clothing (winter coats to underwear), OTC medications, communication aids (cell phones,

CB radios), and downtime games, books, and magazines. They offer copier and fax machine services, sell money orders, provide free microwave use, and of course carry every kind of snack food imaginable. Back beyond the restrooms, one finds a TV lounge and gaming space, a few exercise machines, a laundry area, and showers. In the far reaches of their parking lots, a medical or dental office might be found, also possibly a Mobile Chapel providing "Sunday Services, Counseling and Encouragement." At checkout, their clerks ring up at one low rate coffee in any sized thermos, performing with speed and courtesy. Afterward, they caution everyone to "drive safely." While making announcements over a loudspeaker, they refer to their clientele as "professional drivers."

From my standpoint, the showers provided the biggest surprise. What I had envisioned as similar to the group gym facilities we had in high school turned out to be an unexpected slice of luxury. For a charge, or possibly free if cashing in truck stop reward points, one got an entire modern bathroom, outfitted with every fixture and amenity you might have at home. And it all had been fastidiously cleaned by an attendant right before you were called: "Professional Driver (insert name), your clean shower room is number ..."

Blazing Our Own Trail

We now had come solidly into the Midwest, and because we were making good time toward our target in Wisconsin, Dave decided to leave the interstate and take a lesser highway just to vary the scenery a little. The dispatcher and GPS didn't blurt out any negative reaction, so we proceeded northbound on that foggy morning, passing through tidy farm towns, each marked by a cluster of huge grain elevators. One place, Wilder, Minnesota, listed its population as sixty. During the 1980s, we lived in Minnesota, so this was somewhat familiar territory. We pulled into a truck stop just south of St. Paul, where former neighbors came to take us back to their home for a fun evening of reminiscing and home-cooked food.

Trucker Profile

Many people think in stereotypes, but there's wide variation in the truckers I observed during my road time. They were men, a majority, and women of various races and cultures who ranged in age from younger twenties up to mid-seventies. I would estimate many have education above high school but not much more than an associate's degree, if that. They present in all body shapes and sizes, though many are overweight, some obesely so. When I originally saw handicapped parking slips at truck stops, it seemed these spots might not receive much use. Wrong. We observed numerous truckers who needed this accommodation, evidenced by limited mobility due to age, weight, and/or use of supportive devices. I saw at least one trucker using a portable oxygen machine.

Just as some truckers keep their rigs in nearly spotless condition, as they do their own personal appearance, others look slovenly. They wear a vast array of clothing and footgear. Flip-flops made me look twice, as did a riding companion in a long, flowing skirt and apron. Some look as though they're headed to the gym. They use their off-road time mostly for eating or sleeping, though we observed people cleaning up their cabs, skipping rope, reading the Bible, performing small engine repairs, using their laptops, jogging laps around the lot, and watching TV. Sometimes we'd see a couple of drivers in conversation, though for the most part, they seemed to remain solitary.

Truckin' On

In Wisconsin, we dropped off one load and continued on to Steven's Point for another. Turned out it was Velveeta Cheese. While that origination point made sense (i.e., Wisconsin equals cheese), many of Dave's loads and their destinations questioned logic. As mentioned previously, he carried lots of meat, mostly frozen beef. And frequently, the pickup point was in one cattle-producing state; the load was then packed across one or more similarly producing states, to drop it off farther still in a place that raised its own beef. I know about contracts, selling in volume, and negotiated pricing; still, this whole scheme seemed counterintuitive. Wouldn't some central clearinghouse model where these factors could be run through a formula, allowing equitable compensation for all involved, while putting a priority on local distribution make more sense?

While waiting for our load, another truck pulled up beside us, and out climbed what appeared to be a Muslim couple with two young children, perhaps two and four years old. It was a cold, blustery day, but they walked to the far end of the parking lot and away toward some commercial buildings that must have been a good mile or more removed. I wondered whether the truck was their main home, as it was for some drivers.

So far on that trip, most of the long haulers we'd seen appeared to work alone, though occasionally a team of two would alternate driving. In a truckers' newspaper, I saw a full-page ad seeking spousal driving teams, with the pitch that such an arrangement could cover twice the distance while making twice the money, and, I assume, help combat the social isolation that surely exists.

Congestion and Elements

Outside Milwaukee, a friend met us for breakfast. Long ago, her pastime was driving race cars, so she was all about vehicles of any kind, and from the time she'd met Dave, she endorsed his plan to drive truck. She gave us a quick synopsis of the Wisconsin economy, which had suffered for years with the loss of manufacturing jobs. I asked about the many RV and camper sales lots we passed (not only there but many places in the Midwest), and she summed it up by saying that the state was largely about hunting and fishing.

Heading south toward the end of Lake Michigan, but still possibly fifty miles out from Chicago, traffic started building up considerably, and trucks accounted for a third of it. Getting past this heavy congestion took two to three hours, even though we were traveling mostly at normal highway speeds. Rain and heavy winds buffeted us most of the day, and I could tell that all of it added up to real stress for Dave.

At the truck stop that evening, we did laundry while dodging back and forth to the TV lounge where the NCAA basketball championship game was being viewed by about a dozen men. One in particular loudly trash-talked just about every move by either team. *Like you could do better*, I thought.

Pushing East

Into Ohio, the scenery changed, although we still saw some farmland. Maybe it was because I was reading *Hillbilly Elegy* and sort of knew to look for the signs of economic distress (this was solidly Rust Belt territory), or because now that we'd gone off the interstate and were actually driving through—rather than around—towns and residential areas, we noticed the dowdiness and degree to which more homes were unkempt. Spring had officially arrived, though trees there had not yet begun to leaf out, therefore allowing a peek into yards where one might see collected possessions, everything from rusting lawn furniture to junked cars, scattered in useless disorganization. At Massillon, Ohio, we dropped off the Wisconsin Velveeta, then headed north to pick up some Campbell's soup.

Over the next several days, we partially retraced our route back westward, though on different highways. Along the Indiana Turnpike, we stayed overnight at a rest stop as a departure from the truck stops. The first of these was geared more toward the general traveling population, rather than the latter, which focused on truckers. This one had a huge parking lot, about the only positive aspect of its operation. Inside, all prepared food was dispensed by fast-food chains, and then during quite restricted hours. A mop and bucket stood unattended in the eating area. Somehow the Starbucks that was not open at 7:00 a.m. the following morning seemed consistent with the overall lackadaisical atmosphere. In fairness, we later stayed overnight at a couple of rest stops, state sponsored, that were modern and clean—no food though. Dave actually said that he preferred these, because they were less noisy than most truck stops, which are always twenty-four hours operational.

During his CDL training and again in orientation at Swift, Dave said students were reminded that human trafficking occurs throughout the US, and truckers form a very important link to passing on suspicious situations they may see at truck or rest stops. During my road time, I didn't see anything that might have qualified as this, but then maybe I didn't know what to be watching for either.

Headed West

Once we passed into Iowa, we saw again the orderly farms anchored by barns and small houses with immaculate exteriors. These people seemed to have some kind of unspoken conservancy competition going with their Minnesotan neighbors. Our drop location this time was a massive Walmart Distribution Center. We arrived at 12:40 a.m. to find ourselves almost the sole humans around. Lighting covered the sprawling parking lot but not sufficiently enough to make the slip numbers clearly readable. We crawled along, finally finding our spot, dropped the trailer, and went to look for our next one, a good distance away. While hooking up this new load, Dave remembered he left a padlock on the old one. I was sent to retrieve it in the wind and cold, thankful that at least I had Bob Seger blasting "Old Time Rock and Roll" over loudspeakers.

We progressed into Nebraska, a state that gave frequent veteran recognition on roadside billboards. Its wide-open, largely uninhabited spaces launched us into a conversation we'd had numerous times before. Like everyone else, we heard stories of Americans who had never experienced "The West," or possibly nothing beyond the Appalachian range. Even though we didn't know anyone who fit into that category, we were certain they existed. We imagined those people were from crowded eastern cities and speculated what their reaction would be to places like Nebraska or South Dakota, or even more so to Wyoming. And then taking it from there, we designed a nationwide three- to four-week field trip for such people, covering landmarks like Mt. Rushmore, Las Vegas, the Grand Canyon, Glacier National Park, Santa Fe, Texas, and more. And then one step further, because Dave pondered what his next trucking position would be, we wondered aloud if that was what he should do—haul people around rather than frozen food.

Another frequent discussion we had was our almost certain sense of long-haul truckers' isolation, not only in a physical sense but also politically, philosophically, and culturally. There was nothing I would have rather done than to interview some of those we were encountering to either confirm or deny this assumption, but lacking that, one just had to surmise that continuous long stints away from a home base prevents these drivers from participation in heterogeneous groups or community activities (service groups, HOAs, church congregations, PTAs) that are made up of people possessing various viewpoints. Constant mobility would seem to prevent one from actively participating in forming the guidelines for day-to-day living. It should be mentioned that there are truckers, whether independent or driving for some larger company, who do follow specified routes, so that they can check in at a home base with predicted frequency. But even then, if one is mostly away from that home base, it would seem difficult at best to keep up with community developments and engagement.

Communication

For all the technology Swift Trucking had for creating and tracking our course, somehow mistakes did occur, creating big frustration for drivers. This happened to us in Utah when after following the GPS prompts, we landed in a solidly residential area, unclear where to drop off our load. The work clock was running low too; not much time to find a solution. Similar frustration set in when the company taking delivery was not prepared for it at the designated hour. This day gave Dave grief every which way, because additionally, the truck wasn't moving smoothly. It lurched and chugged along, groaning down the highway at a pace much slower than the rest of traffic. Thankfully, we were not too far from Salt Lake's Swift terminal.

Once there, we had ourselves a sort of housekeeping day because of the extended off-duty clock. First thing was to get the balky engine checked out. We pulled into one of ten work bays and took a seat alongside. Our mechanic traced the problem to the brakes and rapidly cut down an accordion tube while sarcastically muttering, "What kind of a monkey put this thing together!" The replacement process didn't take long, so soon we were parked outside again in a sea of trucks. Dave stayed at that terminal several times before so was familiar with the nearby businesses. They provided the usual offerings that surrounded any large truck terminal—the kind you know must exist, just not the extent to which they do. These include truck and trailer sales yards, accessory dealers, interior repair and upholstery shops, custom trailer design and manufacturers, tire and window sales, safety equipment purveyors, and more. We walked close to a mile through all that to an outdoor mall, where we ate lunch, did a little shopping, and then took in a movie. Afterward, it was back to the truck for a good night's sleep.

Final Leg

We headed across Wyoming, enjoying a much smoother ride thanks to the mechanic's handiwork. This state provided a continuous view of energy production as we traveled eastbound—coal-fired electric plants, wind turbines, gas and oil fields, and some solar panel collection. Lots of agriculture too. Again we saw a steady stream of trucks, which initiated Dave on his ranking commentary. He listed off truck manufacturers Peterbilt, Kenworth, Mack, Volvo, Mercedes, International, Freightliner, and some others. He aspired one day to drive a Kenworth again, as he did with Ed, but for now, he was stuck with a Freightliner, which by his evaluation did not sit in the highest rank of trucks. "Equivalent to a Chevrolet, if you're talking cars," he said. Occasionally, he pointed out fancy paint jobs or certain accessories that he felt distinguished some above the rest. And it may have been these same amenities that pushed some drivers on from simply driving a company truck to becoming an owner/operator; they wanted something that marked their own customization and thereby carried more prestige on the road.

We're tuned in to Wyoming NPR, and their member stations were engaged in a fundraising week. The day's listeners could make pledges in the names of their dogs and cats. Pet Wednesday they termed it. Callers provided varying info about their pets, from the mundane, such as a name, to unusual or annoying habits. And some of them wanted to elaborate in great detail, which thankfully the hosts cut short, but only after securing a pledge. What I thought sounded crazy seemed to work because each hour, they were meeting their goals.

Dave told me that he was planning to submit his letter of resignation once we got to Denver. He had a wonderful few months of driving around the country, but the grind and pressure to constantly be on the road was bearing down. It wasn't exactly the retirement schedule he had in mind. As a sort of culmination, we took a taxi from the truck stop into Laramie and had a delicious dinner in a trendy, casual restaurant. The next day, my ride of a lifetime would end.

Back at Home

A few weeks after resigning from Swift, Dave said to me, "I want to show you the Richie Brothers Auction; it's quite a place." His transparency almost shimmered. Had he hired a plane towing a banner "I want my own truck," his message could not have been clearer. So we went, and it truly is impressive. Acres and acres of not only cabs and trailers of all sorts but heavy-duty construction equipment galore—so much of it that they lend you a golf cart to drive around their sprawling property. On auction days, all of this passes through a large pavilion containing hundreds of spectator seats. Dave registered with them, so now three times each year, he gets their bounteous catalogs, which he carefully studies. He came up with a clever name for his trucking company— still loosely formulated—and loves telling it to anyone appearing to be interested: DLIVERY. And then he had hundreds of business cards with this name followed by his own printed underneath, and he enjoys passing those around. This has evolved into our now receiving business promotions in the mail addressed to DLIVERY, and though he's not interested in those at all, I know he loves seeing that word in print, reinforcing the idea he's made a teeny, tiny impact in the world of trucking.

From the beginning, there's been a range of reaction to this whole undertaking, most of it very positive. One acquaintance called Dave her hero. Conversely, our biscotti-baking neighbor summed it up as "kind of exciting (long pause) but scary." And another friend, believing Dave has simply rounded the bend toward insanity, hugged me and declared, "I just don't know how you deal with him." But no matter where people line themselves up between thinking this is inspired to deranged, everyone wants to go for a ride in the truck.

Wherever all this is headed, I can say without doubt it has been a magnificent adventure. I am so proud that Dave forged his fantasy into being and then let me be a part of it. And no matter how he may continue with this new vocation, whether included or not, I can't imagine ever again being able to bathe in a sparkling clean room that someone else has prepared for me alone—and then beckoned me to it with the classification of "Professional"!

CHAPTER 14
THE END OF THE STORY

SO, THIS STORY now comes to an end. We have provided somewhat different perspectives of the life of a trucker, from a trucker and his wife. As I hope was obvious as you read this book, I have thoroughly enjoyed all aspects of driving truck, from getting to know the truck itself, to learning the rules and habits of the road as a truck driver, and, finally, to experiencing the life and predilections of the many great truck drivers that I met.

Getting to know the truck, both the tractor (what you may call the cab) and the trailer, has been a fascinating experience. From the first day of driver training, learning the eighty-seven discrete parts—from the engine to the brake systems, to the tractor/trailer connections, to the instrument panel, to the gears and the splitter, to the myriad lights and their distinct and unique purposes—all of this has been a great learning experience, particularly for a novice who came to truck driving with very little understanding of the equipment he would be operating. While many drivers I met felt that the daily inspection of equipment (the precheck) was a waste of time, particularly if you were always with the same equipment, I felt it was part of the experience—sort of the process of becoming one with the machine. And while the manuals and handouts could identify and describe each of the pieces of equipment on the truck, those descriptions simply didn't capture the wonder of the hands on review. Bending down and walking under the trailer each morning or after every trailer change to assure that the kingpin was engaged may well have been a pain in the ass for a tall truck driver, but for me at 5'7", it was mostly just fun, as was checking the brakes to ensure that the slack adjusters were appropriately adjusted, if it was for no other reason than to revisit the part with one of the most intriguing names.

Sure, I adopted some shortcuts in the precheck, even some we had been instructed to never take. Perhaps the most significant of these was hitting the tires with a tire thumper, which is either a bat-like club or crowbar (I preferred a crowbar), to check the pressure level of the tires. I admit to taking this shortcut. It certainly wasn't effective in gauging the actual tire pressure, but using a tire gauge every day was tough, time-consuming, and unnecessarily redundant. Whereas, knocking the tires with a club or crowbar worked well in ascertaining whether a tire was actually flat. It may seem strange to hear that a truck driver can't tell that a tire is flat just by looking at it, but you must remember that all tires except the two on the front of the tractor are in tandem, so a flat will be supported by its tandem tire and will look like it is inflated. Hitting the tire with a club of sorts, however, works quite well in alerting a driver to a flat. In my five months of driving with Swift, I had four flat tires, all but one of which I discovered with my crowbar (the fourth was discovered by a mechanic as my rig was being inspected upon arrival at the Swift terminal in Salt Lake City). Twice I passed over selecting an empty trailer because of a flat tire, even though the flat was not clearly visible.

But knowing the equipment is much more than simply doing the precheck and discerning whether the right parts are in place, are properly mounted with clamps or clips tight, and having no cracks, abrasions, cuts, or leaks. Even more important is knowing the role of each part when the truck is in operation. Operating the gears smoothly and learning how to prepare both brakes and gears for steep grades, both climbing and descending, is critically important, as is knowing the rpm ranges within which the gear must be changed and what happens if you miss that gear change. Related to this is learning the dance between braking and gearing in traversing mountain grades. Knowing how to deal with a loss of brakes during operation is equally important.

During the trip on which my wife had joined me for the experience, we lost braking power to both the tractor and trailer while descending a steep grade shortly after passing through Coeur de Lane, Idaho. I still had modest braking capacity but had to rely much more on shifting gears to maintain control, finding an opportune spot to pull off as soon as possible and await arrival of an on-road mechanic to fix a severed brake line. A piece of cloth debris had blown into the area between the tractor and trailer, had caught in the drive train, and spun around, breaking one of the brake lines. While I thought this was probably a freak occurrence, the mechanic assured me that it was rather routine.

Another very simple but oft overlooked maintenance activity is assuring that you have plenty of window cleaner; there is nothing cool about running out of window-cleaning fluid when you are traveling on a slushy highway, with junk being thrown onto the windshield continuously. Another standard task that it took me some time to master was making sure that the turn signal was disengaged after making a turn. Unlike passenger autos, truck tractor turn signals don't go off automatically after a truck makes a turn. I'm sure there is a good reason for this, but it took me some time to get used to turning the signal off, given I hadn't had to worry about this in my BMW. Just like in your car, there is a ticking sound associated with the turn signal, but there is often enough noise in the cab of the tractor to make it difficult to hear the ticking.

While learning the mechanics of truck driving is perhaps the most important initial step in truck driving, learning how to effectively and safely operate the equipment is a second and equally important aspect of driving truck. I've mentioned a couple of operating situations that are very closely related to the mechanics of the truck, but there are other elements of driving that are more purely simple operations. Staying in your lane is perhaps one of the most important because daydreaming or, worse yet, falling asleep because of fatigue can lead a driver to wander a bit from their lane. So, constant vigilance to remaining in your lane is essential to safe driving. And, because you can't actually see exactly where your front tires are on the truck due to the size of the engine compartment, truck drivers also rely heavily on watching their mirrors, from which you can discern more accurately whether or not you are in your lane.

Closely related is the importance of taking great care in changing lanes. The rules of the road call for trucks to stay in the right lane on multilane highways, except when overtaking traffic. Really, this is no different than for four-wheelers, but it is much more likely to be adhered to than is the case for standard autos. As I discussed previously, however, a truck driver must be ever vigilant of traffic behind or beside the truck because there are blind spots that hide traffic on both the left and right sides of the trailer, and you can only be sure that there are no vehicles in the blind spots if you have kept close attention to the traffic following you.

Then, of course, there are those many other unique features of driving a truck that differ fundamentally from driving an auto, from backing at an angle into tight spaces, to turning sharp and narrow corners without cutting off traffic or driving over curbs, to climbing and descending hills, to hitching and disconnecting trailers, and to maintaining sufficient distances behind traffic, despite the efforts of four-wheelers to make that possible, and on and on.

Most of the day (or night) of driving for an over-the-road trucker, however, is simply spent behind the wheel driving at highway speeds across the country. And at least from my perspective, that part of the job is just wonderful. From the hum of the engine and the oneness of driver and truck, to the vistas of the wonderfully diverse geography of this country, driving a truck is simply pure joy, at least for me.

The final aspect of my learning experience, after learning about the mechanics and operations of the truck, was learning about the culture of truck driving. And as humbling as the first two learning experiences were, learning about my fellow truck drivers was perhaps the most humbling. I had spent my entire forty-five-year career as a professional educational policy analyst and administrator. And I had been fortunate to have risen to the highest levels of my profession, including being the CEO of state, federal, and nonprofit organizations. I think it is fair to say that I thought a lot of myself, or as some of my new colleagues probably would say, I was a bit full of myself. And while I was intrigued by the new community of colleagues I was joining, I suspect I came to truck driving thinking I was probably superior to most of those I would be working beside.

I was wrong. I discovered three fundamental elements of the culture of truck driving.

First, there is no single culture of truck drivers. If you want to witness this yourself, pull into a traditional truck stop—a TA, Loves, Pilot, or Flying J—some evening at about dusk and witness the drivers coming in to eat or pick up dinner; use the restroom and maybe take a shower; or nap, chat, or watch TV in the driver's lounge. You will see a population as diverse as America itself—mostly but not exclusively male, less white than you might imagine, with a surprising number of nonnative Americans, including many Eastern Europeans, Middle Easterners, and Mexican and Central Americans, though very few Asians. Furthermore, and part of what I found quite humbling, an awful lot of these folks were very bright. While few were as well educated as me, with my doctorate from Stanford University, many were as articulate, thoughtful, and erudite as I am. My mentor, Ed Gomez, for example—though we had quite different perspectives and opinions on many subjects—was certainly as bright as me and as thoughtful in his approach to life.

Despite having met many very bright truck drivers, the stereotypes actually do fit a lot of drivers. Many are substantially overweight, but that doesn't necessarily distinguish them from many other Americans these days. And while many drivers were very bright, a lot weren't, and I would say that many of those who weren't very bright didn't realize it.

The second element of the truck-driving culture, at least from my perspective, is that, although the community is quite diverse, the nature of the task at hand—driving, usually alone, across the country, with little time off—breeds a loners' culture that focuses almost exclusively on the here and now, with little planning beyond rhetoric for the future, with little awareness of the massive changes occurring in America outside the sphere in which they operate, and with a bit of a victim's attitude. Because drivers interact almost exclusively with others involved with trucking and tend to have little engagement with a traditional community or even with their family, they tend to believe the world is one in which hardworking, regular people like them don't get what they deserve in either earnings or respect. Many, if not most, have little respect for government, though they frankly don't think much about government, and what they do think is that all government is corrupt and impinging on their freedom and liberty. There is little appreciation for the validity of diverse perspectives from individuals or populations with different backgrounds, religions, or educations. In sum, to the extent that there is a truck-driving culture, it is oriented in the present and past, not the future, and it is often driven by self-interest and narrow, ill-informed perspectives. While I have not come to appreciate this general perspective, I have come to understand it better than I did and can now at least understand how good people can support Donald Trump, a perspective I simply did not understand prior to becoming a truck driver.

Third, many truck drivers, like me, love their occupation. Many others, however, despise it. And the difference depends in part on the personalities, in part on their motivations for becoming a truck driver, and in part on maturation.

With respect to personalities, truck driving works best for loners. While I thoroughly enjoyed teaming with Ed during my training and having my wife, Mary Jane, join me, I also enjoy traveling alone in the truck. If you can't enjoy solitude, you shouldn't be a truck driver. And much of the complaining I heard from other drivers focused on this, be it the separation from family and loved ones, the absence of companionship, opinions fostered by isolation, or whatever.

With respect to drivers' different motivations for driving, I heard many who, like me, had always been fascinated by the idea of driving truck, had taken it up, and were living the dream. Others had been equally fascinated, but upon taking up driving had not found it to be what they had hoped for and thus felt trapped in an occupation that was not what they had anticipated. Quite frankly, this is not much different from many other occupations. In my prior life, I met many teachers who thought teaching was going to be one thing, discovered that it was something different, and wanted to get out but couldn't because they were best qualified to be a teacher. Many truck drivers fit this mold. And finally, there are those truckers who went into trucking simply because the high demand for truck drivers meant they could get a job. Some of these weren't very good at anything else and could get a CDL with modest training and then could get a decent-paying job. Not surprisingly, many of these drivers were less than satisfied with their jobs. Others, and there are many of these, came from other countries where they had professional training or highly skilled jobs, but they could not receive recognition in America for that experience and found truck driving to be a good way to make a decent living while they became acclimated to our culture. Surprisingly, I heard very few of these people complain about their jobs. Though many were overqualified for the positions they were in, they recognized it as being part of the process of being an immigrant. Their attitude, in general, seemed to be "it is what it is."

I also witnessed that maturation within the occupation had differential effects on drivers. I truly enjoyed sitting and chatting with those old farts who had driven for their entire lives, who were looking forward to retirement and less back pain but who truly considered themselves as professional drivers and had thoroughly enjoyed their careers. I can't remember a lifer who didn't like her or his job. Now, they often had plenty of complaints, but they were mostly about the new breed of drivers who just didn't get that driving was a privilege and joy. I met others, however, often in the administrative offices of trucking companies, shippers, or receivers, who had simply outgrown driving. Perhaps it was in search of a change of lifestyle, or because of changing family circumstances like marriage and the arrival of children, or simply the evolution of new horizons had led them to move on from being a truck driver. These weren't the ones who left because they weren't fit or pleased to be drivers. These were folks who had enjoyed driving but had come to the point where they needed to move on to something else. Many of these folks found my voyage quite intriguing, because I was doing this in reverse. I had done the professional occupation thing first and picked up driving later on. Many said they envied me, some because they missed the road and others because they thought I could perhaps enjoy the experience more because of my prior work background.

As reflected, I have had a wonderful experience driving truck. I quit driving full-time because there were a number of other things I wished to pursue in retirement, and driving full-time simply didn't provide ample time to do. I purchased, at auction, my own 2013 International ProStar tractor and 2008 Utility trailer and established an LLC from which, for the last two years, I have supported my activities as an independent trucker. My short-lived life as a truck driver, however, is nearing an end. I am approaching celebrating my seventy-fifth birthday (at least to the extent that one can celebrate such events at this age), and though I originally intended to keep driving actively until I was seventy-five, health and wit allowing, I am now retiring from this wonderful gig.

Two factors have contributed to this decision. First, I'm finding it increasingly difficult to find time to drive, given the holiday travel, volunteer activities, desire to golf more, and such, which I find I am enjoying even more than driving. And if I don't drive a reasonable amount, I don't earn enough to pay for insurance, annual licenses and fees, and so on, and it's simply not fair to Mary Jane to spend more of our retirement funds on such an endeavor.

Second, a recent mid-February trip from hell (every driver experiences these) convinced me that maybe I had aged out of this business. The trip was to carry a heavy load from Anheuser Busch's plant in Fort Collins, Colorado, to San Francisco. I had checked the weather, and all looked good, including passage through Donner Pass between Nevada and California, which is notorious for its difficulty and danger for truckers, particularly in the winter. The weather forecasters, however, blew it this time, and the trip was absolutely miserable weather wise. By the time I left Fort Collins, it was already snowing, and by the time I reached I-80 in Wyoming, I was driving through a full-fledged blizzard—heavy snow, strong wind, and black ice. This essentially persisted for two days through Wyoming, Utah, and Nevada until I reached Sparks, Nevada. This included witnessing a truck that had skidded off a pass in Nevada, leaving the trailer hanging off the side of a cliff, with the cab having plunged 250 feet, killing the driver and passenger. This was a sobering moment. I continued on, however, planning on staying the last evening of the trip in Sparks, Nevada, then proceeding to San Francisco the following morning. I really had no choice because Donner by this time was closed to through traffic because of heavy snows (unpredicted), but stopping for the night also gave me the opportunity to get some mechanical assistance I needed before entering California.

Since leaving Colorado, I had been unable to adjust the movable rear tandem axle on my trailer, and I had to move the axle forward to no more than forty-three feet from the fifth wheel assembly connecting the tractor and trailer because that is required in California. So, very weary from two days of tough driving, I pulled into the TA truck stop in Sparks, Nevada, for the evening around 5:00 p.m. I found a wonderful parking spot, parked, and immediately went to the mechanic's shop to line up the repair I needed. They indicated I would be in line and that they hoped to get to me around 8:30 p.m. Well, they actually got around to me at 2:00 a.m. Both they and I thought the problem was probably just that, given the horrendous weather, the rail that rests on the track on which the tandems moved was frozen, but after melting all the ice with a blow torch, we still couldn't move the tandems. We really tried hard, rocking the trailer with the wheels blocked, but to no avail, so they told me I would have to take the trailer to a place that specialized in trailers to get it fixed—and by the way, I needed to get the trailer out of the mechanic's bay so they could work on other trucks.

It was 4:00 a.m. by then, too early to travel to another place, so I proceeded to find a parking place in the TA station, and of course the one I originally had was filled. As I was moving the truck to park it, I heard an unusual, very loud noise, and upon investigating, I discovered that the rail that hung over the track on the rear axle tandem assembly had popped off the track and dropped about a foot, and as a result, the entire assembly had bent. This had also punctured a tire and bent a wheel frame on one of the four tires on the left side of the trailer. This all looked bad, but I didn't realize just how bad.

The following morning, I drove my limping truck half a mile to the recommended trailer specialization shop to discover that it would cost me more than the trailer was worth to repair the damage. As a result, I had to find a replacement truck, trailer, and driver; get my load transferred to assure delivery in San Francisco, at my expense; arrange with my insurance company to salvage my trailer; try to collect my wits; and head back home to Colorado. My return began on a Saturday morning, and I had a pleasant day bob-tailing (which is what driving without a trailer is called) through Nevada and Utah. The blizzard had passed, and the weather was more like I had originally expected. I spent the evening in a truck stop in Fort Bridger, Wyoming, including the required ten-hour break, and headed out Sunday morning for the final trek of this ill-fated journey.

The weather was reasonable except for high winds, and high winds in Wyoming are a truck driver's nightmare. As a truck driver operating originally out of Salt Lake City and later out of Colorado, I often carried loads over I-80 through Wyoming, and winds were almost always an issue, particularly in the winter. I seldom made such a trip without seeing at least one truck that had been blown off the road and was either jackknifed in the median or on its side. And this morning was no different. Less than ten minutes after getting on the road, as I was coming up a hill, I noticed a truck and a car that had been traveling in the opposite lane of the highway off the road crashed in the median. As I came over the hill, I saw seven trucks and two cars that had either been blown off or had slid off the road at the bottom of the hill I had just crested. Some of the trucks were upright, others were on their sides, and a couple were stacked together. Never had I witnessed an accident like this. And none were going anywhere for hours because they were in a very deep snowdrift. I slowed down considerably and passed this disaster, but as I did so, I was thinking, *I'll bet every one of those drivers is much younger than I am at seventy-three, has much quicker reaction times than I do, and probably has much greater driving experience. And, if I had been at this point a few minutes earlier, I would almost certainly have been in that mess with them. Maybe the time has come to say adieu to the joy of truck driving.*

And, indeed, enjoy it I have. My wife, after joining me for three weeks of travel near the end of my tenure with Swift Transportation, said that she thought every American should have to ride across the country in a truck, because they would gain a greater appreciation for the beauty and diversity of this great nation by doing so. Not a bad idea, actually, but I kind of like the fact that this marvelous experience is the unique privilege of those of us who are over-the-road truck drivers. Keep on truckin'!

CPSIA information can be obtained
at www.ICGtesting.com
Printed in the USA
FSHW011958170221
78741FS

9 781665 701143